WILLIAMS-SONOMA

GRILLING

RECIPES AND TEXT
DENIS KELLY

GENERAL EDITOR
CHUCK WILLIAMS

PHOTOGRAPHS
NOEL BARNHURST

SIMON & SCHUSTER • **SOURCE**

NEW YORK • LONDON • TORONTO • SYDNEY • SINGAPORE

CONTENTS

SEAFOOD ON THE GRILL

VEGETABLES ON THE GRILL

SOMETHING SPECIAL

INTRODUCTION

Grilling is one of the most popular ways to cook right now. At any time of year, in any kind of weather, you'll find folks tending the fire, whether it's charcoal or gas. When you think about grilling, certain dishes present themselves: barbecued chicken and ribs, juicy hamburgers and tender steaks. And while this cookbook covers all those classics, it's also full of new ideas that bring grilling up to date. These recipes add the seasonings of Mexican and Asian cuisines where they might not be expected, and bring ingredients like oysters and fruit or dishes like corn bread and pizza to the grill. Today's large grills lend themselves to preparing an entire meal over the fire, and that's just the approach we take in this cookbook.

In addition, each recipe includes a side note on a particular ingredient or technique, giving you in-depth information about the dish, while a chapter of basics covers all you need to know to set up the grill and get started. I hope that this cookbook will help make your outdoor cooking and entertaining more enjoyable.

THE CLASSICS

When you fire up the grill, some foods instantly come to mind: thick and tender steaks, spice-rubbed chicken, and, of course, juicy hamburgers. But in recent years, the repertoire of classic grilled dishes has expanded to include such seafood delicacies as garlicky shrimp and savory smoke-grilled salmon, as well as leg of lamb rubbed with herbs and grilled to succulent perfection.

GRILLED CHICKEN WITH HERB RUB

Prepare a charcoal or gas grill for indirect grilling over medium-high heat (page 107) and oil the grill rack.

To make the herb rub, mix together the paprika, sage, rosemary, garlic powder, cayenne, salt, and black pepper in a small bowl. Coat the chicken with oil and sprinkle generously with the herb rub.

Sprinkle the wood chips on the coals, or add in a perforated foil packet to a gas grill (page 111). Grill the chicken directly over medium-high heat, turning often, until the pieces are well browned, 6–10 minutes total. (Move the chicken to cooler spots on the grill if flare-ups occur.) Transfer the pieces to the unheated portion of the grill, cover the grill, and cook. After 15 minutes, check for doneness by cutting into the chicken at the thickest part or testing with an instant-read thermometer. The chicken should show no sign of pink, and the temperature should reach at least 160°F (71°C). Continue cooking the chicken as needed, up to 10 more minutes, but be careful not to overcook. As the pieces finish cooking (the breasts and/or boneless pieces will be done first), transfer them to a platter and cover loosely with aluminum foil until ready to serve.

Serving Tip: Serve with Garden Skewers (page 83). Grill the skewers over direct heat while the chicken cooks over indirect heat.

MAKES 4 SERVINGS

HERB AND SPICE RUBS

Rubs are dry mixtures of herbs and spices, sprinkled or pressed onto food to flavor it. They can be applied just before grilling or several hours earlier so the food has more time to absorb the rub's flavors. To help a rub adhere, the food may be lightly coated with oil before it is applied. Experiment with your own mixtures, adding or subtracting from the recipe suggested here. Dried herbs such as rosemary, oregano, or thyme are all good additions. Paprika, garlic powder, salt, and pepper are also used in most rubs. Store leftover rub in a sealed jar in a cool, dark place for up to 4 months.

Olive oil or vegetable oil for coating

FOR THE SAGE AND ROSEMARY HERB RUB:

2 tablespoons sweet paprika

2 tablespoons ground sage

1 tablespoon dried rosemary

1 tablespoon garlic powder

½ teaspoon cayenne pepper

1½ teaspoons salt

1 teaspoon freshly ground black pepper

1 chicken, 3–4 lb (1.5–2 kg), cut into serving pieces; 4 bone-in or boneless chicken breast halves; or 12 bone-in or boneless chicken thighs

Wood chips or chunks, soaked for 30 minutes and drained (page 111)

BABY BACK RIBS WITH HONEY-JALAPEÑO MARINADE

FOR THE HONEY-JALAPEÑO MARINADE:

1 cup (8 fl oz/250 ml) vegetable oil

Juice of 2 limes

¼ cup (3 oz/90 g) honey

6 cloves garlic, minced

1 jalapeño chile, seeded and minced

2 tablespoons chopped fresh oregano or 1 table-spoon dried

1 tablespoon sweet paprika

1½ teaspoons salt

1 teaspoon freshly ground pepper

2 racks baby back ribs, about 5 lb (2.5 kg) total, each rack cut into 2 pieces

Wood chips or chunks, soaked for 30 minutes and drained (page 111)

To make the marinade, combine the oil, lime juice, honey, garlic, jalapeño chile, oregano, paprika, salt, and pepper in a small bowl and whisk to blend. Put the ribs in a shallow dish or 1 or 2 large zippered plastic bags and pour the marinade over. Cover or seal and let marinate, turning occasionally, for up to 2 hours at room temperature or overnight in the refrigerator. If refrigerated, remove from the refrigerator 30 minutes before grilling.

Prepare a charcoal or gas grill for indirect grilling over medium-high heat (page 107).

Sprinkle the wood chips on the coals, or add in a perforated foil packet to a gas grill (page 111). Remove the ribs from the marinade and pat dry. Grill the ribs directly over medium-high heat, turning them often, until well browned, 6–10 minutes total. (Move the ribs to cooler spots on the grill if flare-ups occur.) Transfer the seared ribs to the unheated portion of the grill, cover the grill, and cook until they are no longer pink when cut into near the bone and are tender but still juicy, 20–25 minutes longer.

Transfer to a platter, cover loosely with aluminum foil, and let rest for 5 minutes. Cut the ribs apart between the bones to serve.

Serving Tip: For a classic summertime barbecue, serve the ribs with Grilled Corn on the Cob with Chipotle Butter (page 76). You can grill the corn directly over the heat while the ribs finish cooking over indirect heat.

MAKES 4 SERVINGS

RIB CUTS

Baby back ribs are cut from the loin and are the most tender ribs on the market. Look for meaty ribs without much exterior fat. They are excellent grilled after soaking in a tangy marinade. Country-style ribs are cut from the pork shoulder and are meatier and a bit chewier than baby back ribs. They may be substituted in this recipe, although the covered cooking time should be increased by 10–12 minutes. Pork spare-ribs are cut from the belly area and require long, slow, indirect grilling.

SHRIMP WITH LEMON-GARLIC BUTTER

Prepare a charcoal or gas grill for direct grilling over high heat (page 107) and oil the grill rack.

To make the spice rub, mix together the paprika, garlic powder, lemon pepper, and salt in a small bowl.

Coat the shrimp with oil and sprinkle generously with the spice rub. Curl up 1 shrimp, tucking the tail end inside, and thread onto 2 parallel skewers. Repeat with the remaining shrimp, threading 3 shrimp on each pair of skewers.

To make the lemon-garlic butter, melt the butter in a small saucepan over low heat, then stir in the lemon zest and juice, garlic, and cayenne. Pour half of it into a bowl to use for basting and keep the rest warm.

Grill the shrimp directly over high heat, turning once and basting once or twice with the lemon-garlic butter, until evenly pink and opaque throughout, 3–4 minutes on each side. Do not overcook.

Transfer the skewers to a platter. Pour the reserved lemon-garlic butter over the shrimp and serve immediately.

Serving Tips: Serve the shrimp on bruschetta as a first course or over your favorite fresh pasta as a main course. The lemon-garlic butter is also delicious with grilled chicken breasts.

MAKES 4 MAIN-COURSE SERVINGS OR 8 FIRST-COURSE SERVINGS

SHRIMP ON THE GRILL

Shrimp are delicious when brushed with oil or butter, seasoned simply with a spice or herb rub, and then grilled over high heat. They will overcook quickly, however, so keep a close eye on them. As soon as they turn evenly pink on both sides, they are ready. This recipe gives directions for skewering shrimp with 2 skewers, which makes it easy to turn them. Large and jumbo shrimp can be cooked directly on the grill. Or, use a perforated grilling grid, which prevents small pieces of food from falling into the fire.

Olive oil or vegetable oil for coating

FOR THE SPICE RUB:

1 tablespoon sweet paprika

1 tablespoon garlic powder

1 teaspoon lemon pepper or freshly ground black pepper

2 teaspoons salt

24 large shrimp (prawns), about 1 lb (500 g) total weight, peeled and deveined

FOR THE LEMON-GARLIC BUTTER:

½ cup (4 oz/125 g) salted butter

Finely grated zest of 1 lemon

Juice of 1 lemon

4 cloves garlic, minced

¼ teaspoon cayenne pepper, or more to taste

16 wooden skewers, soaked for 30 minutes, or metal skewers

BUTTERFLIED LEG OF LAMB WITH ROSEMARY-GARLIC PASTE

FOR THE ROSEMARY-GARLIC PASTE:

¼ cup (⅓ oz/10 g) minced fresh rosemary or 2 tablespoons dried

8 cloves garlic, chopped

Juice of 2 lemons

2 tablespoons sweet paprika

1 tablespoon salt

1 teaspoon freshly ground pepper

1–2 tablespoons olive oil

1 leg of lamb, 4–5 lb (2–2.5 kg), boned and butterflied (page 110)

To make the rosemary-garlic paste, in a food processor, process the rosemary, garlic, lemon juice, paprika, salt, and pepper with just enough olive oil to make a coarse paste.

Rub the paste generously over both sides of the lamb. Put the lamb in a baking dish or a zippered plastic bag. Cover or seal and let marinate, turning occasionally, for up to 2 hours at room temperature or overnight in the refrigerator. If refrigerated, remove from the refrigerator 30 minutes before grilling.

Prepare a charcoal or gas grill for indirect grilling over medium-high heat (page 107).

Grill the lamb directly over medium-high heat until well browned, turning once, 5–7 minutes on each side. (Move the lamb to a cooler part of the grill if flare-ups occur.) Transfer the lamb, skin side down, to the unheated portion of the grill, cover the grill, and cook. After 30 minutes, check the lamb for doneness by cutting into the thickest part of the meat or testing with an instant-read thermometer. Medium-rare lamb will still be pink inside, and the internal temperature should register 130°–135°F (54°–57°C). Continue cooking as needed, up to 20 minutes more.

Transfer the lamb to a platter, cover loosely with aluminum foil, and let rest for 5 minutes. Slice the meat on the diagonal across the grain and serve.

Serving Tips: Serve with Grilled New Potatoes with a Red Pepper Crust (page 87) and Grilled Red Pepper, Sweet Onion, and Tomato Salad (page 79). The vegetables can be grilled over direct heat while the lamb cooks over indirect heat.

MAKES 6–8 SERVINGS

LEG OF LAMB

While a whole leg of lamb makes a classic Sunday roast, it also takes very well to the grill—if it's boned and butterflied first. Butterflying makes the cut even and allows for relatively quick cooking, which suits flavorful lamb. Simply ask your butcher to bone and butterfly the leg for you, or turn to page 110 for instructions.

SMOKE-GRILLED SALMON WITH FENNEL AND TARRAGON

Prepare a charcoal or gas grill for indirect grilling over medium-high heat (page 107).

If using a salmon fillet, remove any pin bones with sturdy tweezers. Coat the salmon with oil. Cut a piece of heavy-duty aluminum foil large enough to wrap the salmon. If using a whole salmon, place it in the center of the foil and score it 4 or 5 times diagonally through the skin. Put half of the lemon, onion, fennel bulb, and tarragon inside the fish and arrange the rest on top. Sprinkle with the salt and pepper. If using a salmon fillet, place it, skin side down, in the center of the foil and arrange the lemon, onion, fennel, and tarragon down the center. Sprinkle with the salt and pepper. Fold the foil over the salmon and crimp the edges to seal.

Sprinkle the wood chips on the coals, or add in a perforated foil packet to a gas grill (page 111). Place the foil-wrapped salmon on the unheated portion of the grill, cover the grill, and cook. After 35 minutes for whole salmon and 25 minutes for a fillet, open the foil and check for doneness by cutting into the fish or testing with an instant-read thermometer. The salmon should be opaque throughout and flake easily when prodded with a fork, or register 125°F (52°C) on an instant-read thermometer. Continue to cook as needed with the foil opened and the cover on the grill, 10–25 more minutes for whole salmon, 5–15 more minutes for a fillet. Cooking times will vary depending on the size of the fish, the heat of the fire, and the desired degree of doneness. Do not overcook.

Transfer the foil and fish to a large platter. Lift the fish gently with a long spatula and slide the foil out from underneath. Garnish with the reserved fennel tops and serve.

A WHOLE SALMON MAKES 8–10 SERVINGS. A SALMON FILLET 4–6 SERVINGS

1 whole salmon, 5–8 lb (2.5–4 kg), cleaned by the fishmonger, or whole salmon fillet, skin intact, 3–4 lb (1.5–2 kg)

Olive oil or vegetable oil for coating

1 lemon, thinly sliced

1 yellow onion, thinly sliced

1 fennel bulb, trimmed and thinly sliced, feathery green tops reserved for garnish

4 or 5 fresh tarragon sprigs, coarsely chopped, or 1 tablespoon dried tarragon

1 teaspoon salt

½ teaspoon freshly ground pepper

Wood chips or chunks, soaked for 30 minutes and drained (page 111)

SMOKE-GRILLING

Adding hardwood chips or chunks to coals when grilling will infuse food with a delicious smoky flavor. Choose the type of wood to match the food you are grilling. Hickory and oak are intense in flavor and taste best with beef, pork, or chicken. Mesquite, alder, and fruit woods are lighter and can be used with chicken, fish, or shellfish. Soak a handful of chips in water for 30 minutes, then drain and sprinkle them directly on the coals or enclose them in a perforated aluminum foil packet and place on a gas burner just before adding the food.

THE PERFECT HAMBURGER

1 lb (500 g) ground chuck or lean ground beef

2 tablespoons finely chopped yellow onion

1 teaspoon minced garlic

1 teaspoon salt

½ teaspoon freshly ground pepper

1 or 2 dashes of Worcestershire sauce

4 slices Cheddar or Swiss cheese (optional)

4 hamburger buns, split

Sliced tomato for serving

Sliced sweet white onion such as Maui, Vidalia, or Walla Walla for serving

Torn lettuce for serving

Sliced dill pickle for serving

Ketchup, mayonnaise, mustard, or other condiments of your choice

Prepare a charcoal or gas grill for direct grilling over medium-high heat (page 107).

In a large bowl, mix together the beef, onion, garlic, salt, pepper, and Worcestershire sauce. Form the mixture into 4 patties, each ¾ inch (2 cm) thick.

Grill the hamburgers directly over medium-high heat, turning once, 3–5 minutes on each side. Check for doneness by cutting into a hamburger near the center or testing with an instant-read thermometer. No pink should show on the inside (see Note), and the internal temperature should register at least 160°F (71°C). For cheeseburgers, place a slice of cheese on top of each hamburger for the last 3 minutes of cooking.

For the last 2–3 minutes of cooking, toast the hamburger buns, cut side down, on the grill over high heat. Serve the hamburgers on the buns with tomato, onion, lettuce, dill pickle, and condiments.

Note: For health reasons, all ground meat should be cooked at least to the medium-well stage.

MAKES 4 SERVINGS

HAMBURGER VARIATIONS
Use your imagination to jazz up a classic hamburger any way you want. For an Asian twist, omit the Worcestershire sauce and salt, add a dash of soy sauce, and use chopped green (spring) onion instead of yellow onion. For a French hamburger, omit the Worcestershire sauce, halve the salt, and add a table-spoon each of crumbled blue cheese and chopped mush-rooms along with a dash of red wine. For a Provençal flavor, omit the Worcestershire sauce, double the garlic, and add a tablespoon each of chopped dried tomatoes and pitted black olives. Vary the garnishes along with the seasonings.

21

T-BONE STEAKS WITH THREE-PEPPER RUB
AND BOURBON STEAK SAUCE

To make the rub, mix together the black pepper, white pepper, paprika, garlic powder, and salt in a small bowl. Sprinkle the rub generously on both sides of the steaks and press it into the meat. Cover and let sit, turning occasionally, for up to 2 hours at room temperature or overnight in the refrigerator. If refrigerated, remove the steaks from the refrigerator 30 minutes before grilling.

Prepare a charcoal or gas grill for direct grilling over medium-high heat (page 107), leaving a portion of the grill without heat under it.

To make the steak sauce, put the stock in a small saucepan over high heat and boil until reduced by half. In a small bowl, stir the cornstarch into the bourbon. Remove the stock from the heat and whisk in the mustard, tomato paste, cornstarch mixture, and Tabasco. Taste and season with salt. Set aside.

Sprinkle the wood chips on the coals, or add in a perforated foil packet to a gas grill (page 111). Grill the steaks directly over medium-high heat, turning once, 4–7 minutes on each side. (Move the steaks to a cooler portion of the grill if flare-ups occur.) Check for doneness by cutting into a steak near the bone or testing with an instant-read thermometer in the thickest part. Rare steaks will be quite red at the center and register 120°–125°F (49°–52°C); medium-rare will be red to pink and 130°–135°F (54°–57°C); and medium will be just pink and 140°F (60°C). If the steaks are nicely browned but still too rare for your taste, move them to the unheated portion of the grill, cover the grill, and continue cooking as needed. Transfer to a platter, loosely cover with aluminum foil, and let rest for 5 minutes before serving.

Over medium heat, reheat the steak sauce to serving temperature, whisking constantly. Spoon the sauce over the steaks and serve.

MAKES 4 SERVINGS

BOURBON

Cooking with spirits, wine, or beer can add plenty of flavor without adding much alcohol, since most (but not all) of the alcohol boils away in the cooking process. Here, the flavor comes from bourbon, an American whiskey made from corn and aged in charred white-oak barrels that give the liquor a characteristic smoky oak flavor. Other spirits, such as Scotch whisky, Irish whiskey, brandy, rum, or tequila, have their own characters, and each would add its own distinctive touch.

FOR THE THREE-PEPPER RUB:

1 tablespoon freshly ground black pepper

1 tablespoon freshly ground white pepper

1 tablespoon sweet paprika

1 tablespoon garlic powder

2 teaspoons salt

4 T-bone steaks, about 1½ inches (4 cm) thick, trimmed of fat

FOR THE BOURBON STEAK SAUCE:

1 cup (8 fl oz/250 ml) beef stock or canned low-sodium beef broth

1 tablespoon cornstarch (cornflour)

2 tablespoons bourbon

1 tablespoon Dijon mustard

1 tablespoon tomato paste

1 or 2 of dashes of Tabasco or other hot-pepper sauce

Salt

Wood chips or chunks, soaked for 30 minutes and drained (page 111)

MEAT
ON THE GRILL

Beef takes especially well to grilling. There's nothing better than a tender steak, seasoned with herbs and spices, hot from the fire. But other grilled meats are too good to be overlooked: pork tenderloin is delicious grilled and served with a tangy fruit salsa, while thick veal chops seasoned with sage are also excellent fire-roasted.

NEW YORK STRIP STEAKS
WITH THYME AND GARLIC BUTTER

FLAVORED BUTTERS

Flavored butters, also called compound butters, are blends of softened butter with herbs, spices, or other seasonings. They are delicious with grilled fish, chicken, and pork as well as beef. Fresh herbs are especially good when mixed with butter: try tarragon, marjoram, or rosemary. You can also give flavored butters an exotic twist by adding minced ginger, lime or lemon zest and juice, pure chile powder or chopped fresh chiles, or Asian sauces and pastes such as hoisin sauce or black bean or chile paste.

Sprinkle both sides of the strip steaks generously with salt and pepper. Prepare a charcoal or gas grill for direct grilling over medium-high heat (page 107).

To make the thyme and garlic butter, use a fork to blend the butter with the thyme and garlic in a small bowl. Add the Worcestershire and Tabasco sauces to taste. Stir to blend. Set aside or form into a log in waxed paper and refrigerate until ready to use.

Sprinkle the wood chips on the coals, or add in a perforated foil packet to a gas grill (page 111). Grill the steaks directly over medium-high heat, turning 2 or 3 times, until well browned on the outside, 8–12 minutes total. (Move the steaks to a cooler part of the grill if flare-ups occur.) To check for doneness, cut into the steak or test with an instant-read thermometer. Rare steak is red at the center and registers 120°–125°F (49°–52°C); medium-rare is red to pink and 130°–135°F (54°–57°C); medium is pink and 140°F (60°C). Transfer to a platter, loosely cover with aluminum foil, and let rest for 5 minutes.

To serve, spoon 1–2 tablespoons of the flavored butter on top of each steak.

Variation Tip: You may substitute any tender steak suitable for grilling, such as porterhouse or rib eye, in this recipe.

Serving Tip: Serve the steaks with Grilled Corn on the Cob with Chipotle Butter (page 76) and Grilled New Potatoes with a Red Pepper Crust (page 87).

MAKES 4 SERVINGS

4 New York strip steaks, 1½ inches (4 cm) thick, trimmed of fat

Salt and freshly ground pepper

FOR THE THYME AND GARLIC BUTTER:

½ cup (4 oz/125 g) salted butter, at room temperature

1 tablespoon minced fresh thyme or 1½ teaspoons dried

4 cloves garlic, minced

1 or 2 dashes of Worcestershire sauce

1 or 2 dashes of Tabasco or other hot-pepper sauce

Wood chips or chunks, soaked for 30 minutes and drained (page 111)

SKIRT STEAK FAJITAS WITH PICO DE GALLO

½ cup (4 fl oz / 125 ml) vegetable oil

1 yellow onion, thinly sliced

2 cloves garlic, chopped

1 jalapeño chile, minced

1 tablespoon chopped fresh oregano

1 teaspoon ground cumin

1 tablespoon pure chile powder

2 tablespoons chopped fresh cilantro (coriander)

1 tablespoon tequila

1½ teaspoons salt

1 skirt steak or flank steak, 2–3 lb (1–1.5 kg), trimmed of fat and silver skin

FOR THE PICO DE GALLO:

2 tomatoes, coarsely chopped

1 yellow onion, coarsely chopped

¼ cup (⅓ oz/10 g) chopped fresh cilantro (coriander)

1 jalapeño or serrano chile, seeded and minced

Juice of 1 lime

Salt

12 large flour tortillas

In a small bowl, mix together the oil, onion, garlic, chile (remove the seeds and white membranes to cut down on the heat), oregano, cumin, chile powder, cilantro, tequila, and salt. Score the steak a few times across the grain. A long, thin skirt steak should be cut into 2–4 pieces for easy grilling. Put the steak in a baking dish or zippered plastic bag and pour the marinade over. Cover or seal and let marinate, turning occasionally, for up to 2 hours at room temperature or overnight in the refrigerator. If refrigerated, remove from the refrigerator 30 minutes before grilling.

Prepare a charcoal or gas grill for direct grilling over high heat (page 107).

To make the pico de gallo, mix together the tomatoes, onion, cilantro, chile, lime juice, and salt to taste in a bowl. Set aside.

Remove the steak from the marinade and pat dry. Directly over high heat, grill the skirt steak for 3–4 minutes on each side, or the flank steak for 4–5 minutes on each side, turning once. (Move the steak to a cooler part of the grill if flare-ups occur.) Skirt and flank steaks should not be cooked past medium-rare, still slightly pink when cut into at the center, as these cuts toughen when cooked longer. Transfer to a platter and cover loosely with aluminum foil.

Grill the tortillas, turning once, until soft and lightly grill-marked, 2–3 minutes on each side. Slice the steak against the grain into bite-sized pieces. Place the meat on one side of the tortillas, spoon a little pico de gallo on top, and fold. Serve immediately.

Note: The marinade used in this recipe is also delicious with chicken.

MAKES 4–6 SERVINGS

HANDLING CHILES

The heat level of chiles varies dramatically. Large green chiles such as Anaheim or poblano are mild, jalapeños are hot, serranos very hot, and habaneros incandescent. When working with fresh chiles, be careful not to touch your eyes, nose, or mouth, and wash your hands in hot, soapy water afterward. For very hot chiles, use rubber gloves to keep your fingers from burning. To cool the heat, split small hot chiles in half and cut out the seeds and white membranes, which carry most of the heat.

PORK CHOPS
WITH APRICOT-BRANDY GLAZE

Prepare a charcoal or gas grill for direct grilling over medium-high heat (page 107), leaving a portion of the grill with no heat underneath. Oil the grill rack. Score the edge of each chop in a few places to prevent curling.

To make the spice rub, mix together the paprika, garlic powder, thyme, salt, and pepper in a small bowl. Rub generously on both sides of the chops.

To make the glaze, heat the jam in a small saucepan over low heat. Stir in the brandy, mustard, and lemon juice. Set aside, but reheat over medium heat, whisking constantly, just before using.

Grill the chops directly over medium-high heat, turning once, until well browned, 3–4 minutes on each side. Move the chops to the unheated portion of the grill and brush generously with the warm glaze on both sides. Cover the grill and cook for 2–4 minutes more to let the glaze set and the chops finish cooking. Check for doneness by cutting into the chops near the bone or testing the thickest part with an instant-read thermometer. The pork chops should still be just faintly pink inside and register 155°F (68°C). Continue cooking as needed.

Transfer the chops to a platter, loosely cover with aluminum foil, and let rest for 3–5 minutes before serving.

Serving Tip: Serve with Jalapeño Corn Bread (page 101). Make the corn bread before grilling the chops.

MAKES 4 SERVINGS

GLAZING

Brushing meat with a glaze during the last few minutes of grilling creates a beautifully browned surface and adds sweet and savory flavors. Since most glazes contain sugar in some form, be careful about charring and burning. Move food to a cooler part of the grill before applying the glaze and cook over indirect heat to set the glaze. Honey, molasses, fruit jams, port, or sweet sherry are all good sweet additions to glazes, while citrus juices, mustard, chiles, vinegar, or wines are often added for balance.

Olive oil or vegetable oil for coating

8 pork loin or rib chops, bone-in or boneless, at least 1 inch (2.5 cm) thick, trimmed of fat

FOR THE SPICE RUB:

1 tablespoon sweet paprika

1 tablespoon garlic powder

1 teaspoon dried thyme

1½ teaspoons salt

1 teaspoon freshly ground pepper

FOR THE APRICOT-BRANDY GLAZE:

½ cup (5 oz/155 g) apricot jam

2 tablespoons apricot brandy or other brandy

1 tablespoon dry mustard

Juice of 1 lemon

VEAL CHOPS, TUSCAN STYLE

4 large veal loin chops or 8 small veal loin or rib chops, at least 1 inch (2.5 cm) thick, trimmed of fat

2 tablespoons chopped fresh sage or 1 tablespoon dried

4–6 cloves garlic, minced

1½ teaspoons salt, plus more as needed

1 teaspoon freshly ground pepper

1 tablespoon olive oil, or more as needed

1 lb (500 g) dried pasta such as penne

Grilled-Tomato Sauce *(far right)* for topping

Score the edge of each chop in a few places to prevent curling. In a small bowl, mix together the sage, garlic to taste, salt, pepper, and enough olive oil to make a thick paste. Rub both sides of the chops generously with the herb paste. Let the chops sit at room temperature for up to 1 hour before grilling.

Prepare a charcoal or gas grill for direct grilling over medium-high heat (page 107), leaving a portion of the grill with no heat underneath. Oil the grill rack.

Fill a large pot three-quarters full of water and bring to a boil over high heat.

Grill the chops directly over medium-high heat, turning once, until well browned, 3–5 minutes on each side. Check for doneness by cutting into the chops at the bone or testing with an instant-read thermometer in the thickest part. The veal chops should be lightly pink at the bone and should register 150°F (65°C). If the chops are well browned but still undercooked on the inside, move them to the unheated portion of the grill, cover the grill, and continue to cook as needed. Transfer the chops to a platter, loosely cover with aluminum foil, and let rest for 5 minutes.

Meanwhile, salt the boiling water and add the pasta. Cook until al dente and drain.

Put 1 or 2 chops on each plate and top with a large spoonful of the grilled-tomato sauce. Mix the rest of the sauce with the pasta and serve alongside the chops.

MAKES 4 SERVINGS

GRILLED-TOMATO SAUCE
Grilling intensifies the flavor of sweet summer tomatoes. Brush 4 large or 8 small tomatoes with olive oil. Grill the tomatoes directly over medium-high heat, turning often, until they are grill-marked on all sides and starting to soften, 5–8 minutes. Don't worry if they char a bit, but take care not to overcook them. Transfer to a cutting board, cut out the stems, and chop the tomatoes coarsely. Put the tomatoes in a bowl and stir in 2–3 cloves minced garlic, 2 tablespoons chopped fresh basil, and salt and pepper to taste. The sauce is wonderful on grilled pizza (page 90).

HERB-CRUSTED RACK OF LAMB
WITH MINT AND SHERRY GRAVY

In a small bowl, mix together the thyme, garlic, salt, and pepper. Add just enough olive oil to make a thick paste. Rub the paste all over the lamb and let sit for up to 1 hour at room temperature.

Prepare a charcoal or gas grill for indirect grilling over high heat (page 107).

To make the gravy, preheat the oven to 400°F (200°C). Put the lamb trimmings in an ovenproof frying pan and roast until they render their fat, 15–20 minutes. Using a slotted spoon, remove the solids from the pan. Pour off all but 2 tablespoons of the fat, or, if you don't have lamb trimmings, melt the butter in a frying pan. Place over medium heat, stir the flour into the lamb fat or butter, and cook, stirring constantly, until fragrant but not colored, 1–2 minutes. Whisk in the stock, sherry, tomato paste, mint, oregano, and salt and pepper to taste. Cook, whisking often, until thickened and smooth, 3–5 minutes. Add the vinegar and, if desired, Tabasco to taste. Set aside and keep warm.

Grill the lamb directly over high heat, fat side down, until well browned, 7–10 minutes. (Move it to a cooler portion of the grill if flare-ups occur.) Place the racks fat side up on the unheated portion of the grill, cover the grill, and cook. After 15 minutes, check for doneness by cutting into the meat next to the bone or inserting an instant-read thermometer into the thickest part. Medium-rare lamb will be red to pink near the bone and should register 130°–135°F (54°–57°C). Continue cooking the lamb as needed, up to 10 minutes more. Transfer to a platter, loosely cover with aluminum foil, and let rest for 5–10 minutes.

Cut the racks into chops. Place 2 chops on each plate, spoon the gravy over the chops, and pass the remaining gravy at the table.

MAKES 4 SERVINGS

FRENCHING LAMB

Trimming a rack of lamb before cooking is a technique called Frenching. Ask your butcher to do this, or do it yourself: With a sharp boning knife, cut away the meat and fat between each rib bone to expose 1–2 inches (2.5–5 cm) of bone at the top of the rack. Trim off most of the fat from the loin meat and score the remaining fat in a crisscross pattern. If desired, wrap the tips of the bones in foil to prevent charring. Carving will be easier if the butcher saws through the chine bone along the bottom between each chop.

¼ cup (⅓ oz/10 g) minced fresh thyme

6 cloves garlic, minced

1 tablespoon salt

1 teaspoon ground pepper

1–2 tablespoons olive oil

2 racks of lamb (about 1 lb/500 g each), trimmed and Frenched *(far left)*, trimmings reserved

FOR THE GRAVY:

Reserved trimmings from lamb, *above*, or 2 tablespoons unsalted butter

2 tablespoons flour

1 cup (8 fl oz/250 ml) beef or vegetable stock

½ cup (4 fl oz/125 ml) medium-dry sherry

1 tablespoon tomato paste

1 tablespoon chopped fresh mint

1 tablespoon chopped fresh oregano

Salt and ground pepper

1 teaspoon balsamic vinegar

1 or 2 dashes of Tabasco or other hot-pepper sauce (optional)

LAMB AND MUSHROOM KABOBS

FOR THE MARINADE:

Juice of 1 lemon

¼ cup (2 fl oz / 60 ml) olive oil

1 tablespoon red wine vinegar

2 tablespoons minced fresh oregano or 1 table-spoon dried

1 yellow onion, chopped

4 cloves garlic, minced

1½ teaspoons salt

1 teaspoon freshly ground pepper

2 lb (1 kg) boneless lamb from leg or shoulder, trimmed of fat and cut into 1½-inch (4-cm) cubes

32 cremini or white button mushrooms, whole or cut into 1½-inch (4-cm) pieces

8–12 wooden skewers, soaked for 30 minutes, or metal skewers

To make the marinade, mix together the lemon juice, oil, vinegar, oregano, onion, garlic, salt, and pepper in a small bowl. Place the lamb in a bowl or zippered plastic bag and pour the marinade over. Cover or seal and let marinate, turning occasionally, for up to 2 hours at room temperature or overnight in the refrigerator. If refrigerated, remove from the refrigerator 30 minutes before you plan on grilling.

Prepare a charcoal or gas grill for direct grilling over medium-high heat (page 107).

Remove the lamb cubes from the marinade and pat dry, reserving the marinade. To make the kabobs, thread the pieces of lamb alternately with the mushrooms on the skewers. Brush with the reserved marinade.

Grill the skewers directly over medium-high heat, turning often, until well browned, 5–7 minutes total. (Move the skewers to a cooler part of the grill if flare-ups occur.) Check for doneness by cutting into a kabob or testing with an instant-read thermometer. The meat should still be pink to red at the center and should register 130°–135°F (54°–57°C). Continue to cook the skewers as needed. Transfer to a platter, cover loosely with aluminum foil, and let rest for 3–5 minutes before serving.

Serving Tip: Serve the skewers on a bed of rice pilaf accompanied with Grilled Red Pepper, Sweet Onion, and Tomato Salad (page 79). Grill the vegetables and make the salad before grilling the lamb.

MAKES 4–6 SERVINGS

KABOB VARIATIONS

Lamb is the traditional meat used to make kabobs, an age-old preparation that originated in the Middle East. But other meats, vegetables, and even tofu can also be used. Try cubes of beef tenderloin seasoned with a spice rub and skewered with pieces of red and yellow bell pepper (capsicum), or chunks of pork tenderloin with pieces of pineapple and sweet onion. And, for an alternative way of serving, remove the meat and vegetables after grilling and tuck them into warm pita bread.

FLANK STEAK WITH GINGER MARINADE

FRESH GINGER

Fresh ginger is found in nearly every supermarket produce section nowadays. Preparing it is simple: Break off a piece the size you need, use a paring knife or vegetable peeler to remove the thin beige skin, and then cut or grate as directed in individual recipes. Some cooks like to wrap minced ginger in cheesecloth (muslin) or a kitchen towel and wring out the juice for use in marinades and sauces. Fresh ginger will keep for up to 3 weeks in a plastic bag in the vegetable drawer of the refrigerator. Use it in salsas, salad dressings, and stir-fries or wherever you want its tangy, lively taste.

Score the flank steak about ¼ inch (6 mm) deep across the grain 3 or 4 times on both sides.

To make the marinade, mix together the soy sauce, mirin, peanut and sesame oils, ginger, green onion, garlic, and chile oil in a small bowl. Put the steak in a baking dish or a zippered plastic bag and pour the marinade over. Cover or seal and let sit, turning occasionally, for up to 2 hours at room temperature or overnight in the refrigerator. If refrigerated, remove from the refrigerator 30 minutes before grilling.

Prepare a charcoal or gas grill for direct grilling over medium-high heat (page 107).

Remove the steak from the marinade and pat dry. Grill directly over medium-high heat, turning it 2 or 3 times, until well browned, 6–10 minutes total. (Move the steak to a cooler part of the grill if flare-ups occur.) Check for doneness by cutting into the meat or testing it with an instant-read thermometer. Rare steak is red at the center and registers 120°–125°F (49°–52°C); medium-rare is red to pink at the center and 130°–135°F (54°–57°C), medium is pink and 140°F (60°C). Don't cook flank steak past medium, or the meat will toughen. Transfer to a platter, loosely cover with aluminum foil, and let rest for 5 minutes. To serve, slice it into thin diagonal slices against the grain.

Note: Mirin, a Japanese sweet rice wine for cooking, and sake can be found in Asian markets or the Asian section of many supermarkets.

Serving Tip: Serve with Wild Mushroom Quesadillas (page 84) and Garden Skewers (page 83).

MAKES 4–6 SERVINGS

1 flank steak, 2–3 lb (1–1.5 kg), trimmed of fat and silver skin

FOR THE GINGER MARINADE:

¼ cup (2 fl oz/60 ml) soy sauce

¼ cup (2 fl oz/60 ml) mirin, sake, or sweet sherry (see Note)

½ cup (4 fl oz/125 ml) peanut oil or vegetable oil

1 tablespoon Asian sesame oil

¼ cup (1 oz/30 g) peeled and minced fresh ginger

¼ cup (1 oz/30 g) finely chopped green (spring) onion, including tender green parts

4 cloves garlic, minced

1 tablespoon chile oil or chile paste

BUTTERFLIED PORK TENDERLOINS WITH MANGO-LIME SALSA

FOR THE SMOKY SPICE RUB:

2 tablespoons pure chile powder, preferably chipotle

1 tablespoon garlic powder

1 teaspoon onion powder

1 teaspoon dried sage

1½ teaspoons salt

2 pork tenderloins, about 1½ lb (750 g) each, trimmed of fat and silver skin

Olive oil or vegetable oil for coating

Mango-Lime Salsa (far right) for serving

Wood chips or chunks, soaked for 30 minutes and drained (page 111)

To make the spice rub, mix together the chile powder, garlic powder, onion powder, dried sage, and salt in a small bowl.

Cut each tenderloin in half crosswise. Butterfly the 4 pieces by cutting them halfway through lengthwise. Open each piece like a book and pound with the flat side of the knife or a cleaver to flatten it. Coat the pork with oil on both sides and sprinkle generously with the spice rub. Place in a baking dish, cover, and let sit, turning occasionally, for 2 hours at room temperature or overnight in the refrigerator. If refrigerated, remove from the refrigerator 30 minutes before grilling.

Prepare a charcoal or gas grill for direct grilling over medium-high heat (page 107), leaving a portion of the grill with no heat underneath. Oil the grill rack.

Sprinkle the wood chips on the coals, or add in a perforated foil packet to a gas grill (page 111). Grill the tenderloins directly over medium-high heat, turning once, until well browned, 4–5 minutes on each side. Check for doneness by cutting into the center or testing with an instant-read thermometer. The pork should be just faintly pink at the center and the internal temperature should register 155°F (68°C). If the tenderloins are well browned but still undercooked, move them to a cooler part of the grill, cover the grill, and continue to cook as needed.

Transfer the pork to a platter, loosely cover with aluminum foil, and let rest for 5–10 minutes. To serve, cut against the grain into diagonal slices and accompany with the salsa.

Serving Tip: Serve with Wild Mushroom Quesadillas (page 84).

MAKES 4 SERVINGS

MANGO-LIME SALSA

Tangy, colorful, and easy to make, fruit salsas are excellent accompaniments to grilled meat, poultry, or fish.
To make mango-lime salsa, combine 2 diced mangoes, 1 diced ripe yellow tomato, 1 diced sweet onion, the juice of 1 lime, 1 minced seeded serrano or jalapeño chile, 2 tablespoons chopped fresh mint, 1 tablespoon honey, and 2 teaspoons salt in a bowl. The salsa can be made up to 2 hours before serving. You can also substitute ripe peaches, apricots, pineapple, or papaya for the mangoes.

POULTRY ON THE GRILL

Barbecued chicken is a favorite, but it's a dish that's not always well prepared. The trick is to cook it all the way through without letting the meat dry out or the skin char. The recipes that follow ensure tender and savory results every time, and bring turkey, duck, and game hens to the grill as well, with very tasty results.

GRILLED CHICKEN WITH HOME-STYLE BARBECUE SAUCE

To make the herb rub, mix together the paprika, garlic powder, oregano, rosemary, salt, and pepper in a small bowl. Sprinkle generously all over the chicken pieces, rub in, and let sit at room temperature for up to 1 hour.

Prepare a charcoal or gas grill for indirect grilling over medium-high heat (page 107).

Sprinkle the wood chips on the coals, or add in a perforated foil packet to a gas grill (page 111). Grill the chicken directly over medium-high heat, turning once, until well browned, 3–5 minutes on each side. (Move the chicken to cool spots on the grill if flare-ups occur.) Transfer the pieces to the unheated portion of the grill, cover the grill, and cook for 5 minutes. Brush both sides of the chicken pieces liberally with barbecue sauce and cook for 5 more minutes. Check for doneness by cutting into the chicken near the bone or testing with an instant-read thermometer. The chicken should show no sign of pink, and the temperature should reach at least 160°F (71°C). Continue cooking as needed. As the pieces finish cooking (the breasts will be done first), transfer them to a platter and cover loosely with aluminum foil until ready to serve.

Note: Be sure to boil any barbecue sauce that has come in contact with raw chicken. This includes any sauce remaining in the bowl after the chicken has been basted during cooking. The used basting brush should be washed with soap and hot water before being used again to apply sauce to cooked chicken. Leftover sauce can be covered and refrigerated for up to 2 weeks.

Serving Tip: Serve with Grilled Corn on the Cob with Chipotle Butter (page 76) and Grilled Red Pepper, Sweet Onion, and Tomato Salad (page 79).

MAKES 4 SERVINGS

BARBECUE SAUCE

Here's an easy barbecue sauce to be brushed onto chicken, pork, or beef during the last few minutes of cooking. In a sauce-pan over low heat, whisk 2 cups (16 oz/500 g) ketchup with ¼ cup (2 fl oz/60 ml) distilled white vinegar; ¼ cup (2½ oz/75 g) molasses; 1 tablespoon dry mustard; 1 tablespoon pure chile powder; 1 teaspoon *each* ground cumin, dried oregano, and freshly ground pepper; and 2 tablespoons bourbon (optional). Simmer for 20–30 minutes, stirring often. Add salt and Tabasco to taste. Makes about 2½ cups (20 oz/625 g).

FOR THE HERB RUB:

1 tablespoon sweet paprika

1 tablespoon garlic powder

1 tablespoon dried oregano

1 teaspoon dried rosemary

1½ teaspoons salt

1 teaspoon freshly ground pepper

1 chicken, 2½–3 lb (1.25–1.5 kg), quartered; 4 bone-in chicken breast halves; or 8 bone-in chicken thighs

Barbecue Sauce *(far left)* for brushing

Wood chips or chunks, soaked for 30 minutes and drained (page 111)

CORNISH HENS UNDER A BRICK, ITALIAN STYLE

FOR THE MARINADE:

2 cups (16 fl oz/500 ml) olive oil

¼ cup (2 fl oz/60 ml) balsamic vinegar

6 cloves garlic, chopped

2 tablespoons minced fresh basil or 1 tablespoon dried

2 tablespoons minced fresh oregano or 1 tablespoon dried

1 teaspoon hot red pepper flakes

Juice of 1 lemon

1 tablespoon salt

2 teaspoons freshly ground black pepper

4 Cornish game hens, split down the back and flattened, or 2 poussins or small chickens, halved

4 clean bricks or other weights, wrapped in aluminum foil

Wood chips or chunks, soaked for 30 minutes and drained (page 111)

To make the marinade, mix together the oil, vinegar, garlic, basil, oregano, red pepper flakes, lemon juice, salt, and black pepper in a small bowl. Put the game hens or poussin halves in a baking dish or zippered plastic bags and pour the marinade over. Cover or seal and let sit, turning occasionally, at room temperature for up to 2 hours or overnight in the refrigerator. If refrigerated, remove from the refrigerator 30 minutes before grilling.

Prepare a charcoal or gas grill for indirect grilling over medium-high heat (page 107).

Sprinkle the wood chips on the coals, or add in a perforated foil packet to a gas grill (page 111). Remove the birds from the marinade and pat dry. Place them on the grill directly over medium-high heat, skin side up, and place a foil-covered brick on each one. Grill until well browned on the bottom side, 5–7 minutes, moving the birds to cooler parts of the grill if flare-ups occur. Turn the hens over, replace the bricks, and grill until the skin side is well browned, another 5 minutes. Remove the bricks and place the hens on the unheated portion of the grill, skin side up. Check for doneness by cutting into the hens next to the thigh bone or testing with an instant-read thermometer in the thickest part. The hens should not show any pink near the bone and should register at least 160°F (71°C). Cover the grill and continue cooking as needed, 10–15 minutes more.

Transfer the birds to a platter, cover loosely with aluminum foil, and let rest for 5 minutes before serving.

Serving Tip: Serve whole game hens or poussin halves with pasta topped with Grilled-Tomato Sauce (page 33). Make the sauce before you grill the birds.

MAKES 4 SERVINGS

HENS UNDER A BRICK
This Italian grilling method flattens poultry and holds it uniformly against the grill so it cooks quickly and evenly. Use the same technique for any split small birds, such as quail, squab, or guinea hens. Pork chops or pork tenderloins can also be cooked under a weight so that they don't curl up on the grill. Bricks, river stones, metal pounding tools, and other weights all work well. Don't use canned foods as weights, however, as the heat could cause them to explode.

CHICKEN BREASTS STUFFED WITH FRESH SAGE AND MOZZARELLA

Prepare a charcoal or gas grill for direct grilling over medium-high heat (page 107) and oil the grill rack.

Using a long, thin, sharp knife, butterfly the chicken breasts: Cut horizontally into the thickest part of each breast to within ½ inch (12 mm) of the other side. Open the breast like a book and place it between sheets of plastic wrap. Pound lightly with the flat side of a cleaver or knife to flatten and even out the thickness. Remove the top sheet of plastic wrap and lay 1 slice of cheese and 2 sage leaves on one half of the flattened breast. Sprinkle with salt and pepper and fold the chicken over the cheese. Coat with oil and sprinkle both sides with salt and black pepper. Repeat with the remaining chicken breasts and filling.

To make the sage butter, with a fork, mix together the butter, sage, garlic, and cayenne in a small bowl and blend well. Set aside or form into a log in waxed paper and refrigerate until ready to use.

Grill the chicken on one side directly over medium-high heat for 3–5 minutes, then turn carefully with a spatula. Grill on the second side for 3 minutes. Check for doneness by cutting into the center of one of the breasts. There should be no pink showing. Cook longer if necessary, but be careful not to overcook them, as chicken breasts dry out and toughen if cooked too long.

Top each breast with 1 tablespoon or more sage butter and serve.

Serving Tip: Make a double portion of sage butter and toss the extra with cooked pasta. Serve the chicken breasts alongside or on top of the pasta, garnished with fresh sage leaves.

MAKES 4 SERVINGS

Olive oil or canola oil for coating

4 boneless, skinless chicken breast halves

4 slices mozzarella cheese

8 fresh sage leaves

Salt and freshly ground black pepper

FOR THE SAGE BUTTER:

½ cup (4 oz/125 g) salted butter, at room temperature

1 tablespoon chopped fresh sage

2 cloves garlic, minced

¼ teaspoon cayenne pepper

CHILE-STUFFED TURKEY THIGHS

4 boneless, skin-on turkey thighs (see Note)

1 can (7 oz/220 g) chipotles en adobo *(far right)*

1 cup (4 oz/120 g) shredded Monterey jack cheese

1 Anaheim or other mild green chile, roasted and peeled (page 114), then chopped

1 tablespoon pure chile powder

Salt

Olive oil or vegetable oil for coating

Spread out the thighs, skin side down, on a work surface. Put 1 or 2 chipotles (remove the seeds to lessen the heat a bit) down the center of each thigh, and top each with ¼ cup (1 oz/30 g) shredded cheese and one-fourth of the chopped green chile. Roll the thighs up around the chiles and cheese and tie in 2 or 3 places with kitchen string. Brush the outsides of the thighs with adobo sauce from the can and sprinkle with chile powder and salt. Cover and let marinate for up to 2 hours at room temperature or overnight in the refrigerator. If refrigerated, remove from the refrigerator 30 minutes before grilling.

Prepare a charcoal or gas grill for indirect grilling over medium-high heat (page 107) and oil the grill rack.

Grill the thighs, skin side down, directly over medium-high heat until well browned, 5–7 minutes. (Move them to a cooler area of the grill if flare-ups occur.) Turn and transfer to the unheated portion of the grill. Cover the grill and cook for another 12–15 minutes. Check for doneness by cutting into the center of a thigh or testing with an instant-read thermometer. The turkey should show no pink and should register at least 160°F (71°C). Continue to cook as needed. Transfer to a platter, cover loosely with aluminum foil, and let rest for 5 minutes before serving.

Note: If you cannot find boneless turkey thighs, bone them yourself by running a thin, sharp knife down the inside of the thigh bone and lifting it out, keeping the meat in 1 piece.

Serving Tip: Serve with Wild Mushroom Quesadillas (page 84). Grill the quesadillas over direct heat while the turkey thighs cook over indirect heat or rest before serving.

MAKES 4 SERVINGS

CHIPOTLES

Chipotles are ripe red jalapeño chiles that have been dried and smoked. They are available in Latin groceries, but the best way to buy them for this recipe is canned and packed in adobo sauce, a tangy blend of tomato and onion. Canned chipotles en adobo may be found in most supermarkets. Use the chiles wherever you want some smoke and heat, and add a splash of adobo sauce to flavor sauces for grilled chicken, fish, or pork.

GRILLED DUCK BREASTS WITH
DRIED CHERRY–ZINFANDEL SAUCE

Prepare a charcoal or gas grill for direct grilling over medium heat (page 107).

To make the spice rub, mix together the ginger, five-spice powder, white pepper, and salt in a small bowl. Sprinkle generously on both sides of the duck breasts and rub in.

To make the sauce, combine the stock, wine, dried cherries, soy sauce, and corn syrup in a saucepan. Cook over high heat, stirring often, until reduced by about half, 7–10 minutes. Remove from the heat. Stir in the cornstarch mixture and cook over medium heat for about 1 minute, stirring constantly, to thicken the sauce. Set aside and keep warm.

Place the duck breasts on the grill, skin side down, directly over medium heat. Cover the grill and cook until the duck is well browned on the bottom side, 7–10 minutes, checking occasionally for flare-ups and moving the poultry to a cooler part of the grill if needed. Turn and grill for 5 minutes longer. Check for doneness by cutting into a breast or testing with an instant-read thermometer. Duck breasts should be cooked medium-rare to medium, still pink at the center, or until an instant-read thermometer registers 135°–140°F (57°–60°C). Continue to cook as needed.

Transfer to a platter, cover loosely with aluminum foil, and let rest for 5 minutes. To serve, slice each duck breast on the diagonal and serve with the sauce spooned over.

Note: The spice rub in this recipe is also delicious with chicken or pork.

Serving Tip: Serve over rice with Grilled Portobello Mushrooms with Basil Oil (page 80).

MAKES 4 SERVINGS

PAIRING DUCK
AND FRUIT

This recipe pairs dried cherries with duck, but other dried fruits would work equally well in a wine-based sauce served with this game bird, with quail or pheasant, or with pork or smoked ham. Instead of the dried cherries with Zinfandel used here, try dried cranberries with Pinot Noir, dried peaches or apricots with Riesling or Gewürztraminer, dried pears with Sauvignon Blanc, or dried apples with Chardonnay, varying spices and herbs as you wish.

FOR THE SPICE RUB:

1 tablespoon ground ginger

1 tablespoon Chinese five-spice powder

1 tablespoon freshly ground white pepper

1½ teaspoons salt

4 boneless, skin-on duck breast halves

FOR THE SAUCE:

1 cup (8 fl oz/250 ml) chicken stock or canned low-sodium chicken broth

¼ cup (2 fl oz/60 ml) Zinfandel or other full-bodied dry red wine

½ cup (2 oz/60 g) dried sweet cherries

1 tablespoon dark soy sauce

1 tablespoon dark corn syrup

1 tablespoon cornstarch (cornflour) dissolved in 2 tablespoons wine or water

WHOLE GRILL-ROASTED TURKEY

FOR THE CHILE SPICE RUB:

¼ cup (¾ oz/20 g) pure chile powder

2 tablespoons sweet paprika

1 tablespoon dried oregano

1 teaspoon ground cumin

1 teaspoon dried rosemary

1 tablespoon salt

½ teaspoon cayenne pepper

1 small turkey, 8–12 lb (4–6 kg), or 2 large chickens, 4–6 lb (2–3 kg) each

Olive oil or vegetable oil for coating

Wood chips or chunks, soaked for 30 minutes and drained (page 111)

To make the spice rub, mix together the chile powder, paprika, oregano, cumin, rosemary, salt, and cayenne in a small bowl.

Rub the turkey with oil, sprinkle the spice rub generously all over the bird, and rub it in. If any is left over, rub it inside the cavity.

Prepare a charcoal or gas grill for indirect grilling over medium-high heat (page 107). If you have a rotisserie setup for your grill, this is a good dish to cook on a spit *(right)*.

Sprinkle the wood chips on the coals, or add in a perforated foil packet to a gas grill (page 111). Roast the turkey or chickens over indirect heat or on a spit in a covered grill for about 1 hour for turkey, 45 minutes for chicken. Check occasionally to make sure the skin is not getting too brown and cover the breast loosely with aluminum foil if necessary. If using a spit, turn the heat down on a gas grill or use tongs to remove a few coals from a charcoal fire to lower the heat level; add more coals as needed to replenish the fire. After 45 minutes, check for doneness by cutting into the inside of the thigh next to the bone or testing with an instant-read thermometer in the thickest part. The turkey or chicken should not show any pink next to the bone and should register at least 160°F (71°C). Continue to cook as needed. Transfer to a platter, cover loosely with aluminum foil, and let rest for 15 minutes for turkey, 10 minutes for chicken. Carve and serve.

Serving Tip: Serve with Grilled Corn on the Cob with Chipotle Butter (page 76), Grilled New Potatoes with a Red Pepper Crust (page 87), and Jalapeño Corn Bread (page 101). Bake the corn bread before grilling the bird, then grill the vegetables over direct heat while the bird cooks over indirect heat or rests before serving.

MAKES 6–8 SERVINGS

SPIT-ROASTING

Roasting on a spit is an ideal way to cook a small turkey or a couple of chickens. It's a good idea to tie the legs of the bird together and to truss the wings. This makes for a more manageably shaped bird to attach to the spit. Then, run the spit through the cavity, driving one of the spit forks into the thighs and the other into the breast. The trick with spit-roasting is to balance the food on the spit so that it turns smoothly and evenly. Many rotisserie sets include counter-weights, which help with this.

CHICKEN SATAY WITH PEANUT SAUCE

To make the marinade, mix together the oil, lime juice, garlic, green onions, ginger, soy sauce, and chile oil in a small bowl.

Put the chicken chunks in a baking dish or zippered plastic bag and pour the marinade over. Cover or seal and let sit, turning occasionally, for up to 2 hours at room temperature or overnight in the refrigerator. If refrigerated, remove from the refrigerator 30 minutes before grilling.

Prepare a charcoal or gas grill for direct grilling over medium-high heat (page 107).

Remove the chicken from the marinade, pat dry, and thread onto the skewers. Grill the skewers directly over medium-high heat, turning once, until well browned, 4–5 minutes on each side. Check for doneness by cutting into a piece of chicken. It should show no pink at the center.

Serve the skewers over the cooked white rice, topped with warm peanut sauce.

Variation Tips: Pork tenderloin or beef flank steak may be used in this recipe. Pork should be cooked to 155°F (68°C), flank steak to 125°F (52°C). Adjust cooking times accordingly.

MAKES 4 SERVINGS

PEANUT SAUCE

To make peanut sauce, heat 2 tablespoons peanut oil or vegetable oil in a nonaluminum saucepan over medium-high heat. Add ¼ cup (1 oz/30 g) chopped green (spring) onions, including tender green parts, and sauté until translucent, 2–3 minutes. Stir in ½ cup (5 oz/155 g) creamy peanut butter, ½ cup (4 fl oz/125 ml) chicken stock or canned low-sodium broth, 1 teaspoon sugar, the juice of ½ lemon, 1 tablespoon soy sauce, and ¼ cup (1 oz/30 g) chopped peanuts. Simmer over low heat for 10 minutes, stirring often. Add Asian chile sauce to taste.

FOR THE MARINADE:

½ cup (4 fl oz/125 ml) peanut oil or vegetable oil

Juice of 1 lime

4 cloves garlic, minced

¼ cup (1 oz/30 g) chopped green (spring) onions, including tender green parts

2 tablespoons peeled and minced fresh ginger

2 tablespoons soy sauce

1 teaspoon Asian chile oil or sauce, or to taste

1 lb (500 g) boneless, skinless chicken thighs, trimmed of fat and cut into 1-inch (2.5-cm) chunks

1½ cups (10½ oz/330 g) white rice, cooked according to package directions, for serving

Peanut Sauce *(far left)* for serving

8 wooden skewers, soaked for 30 minutes, or metal skewers

SEAFOOD
ON THE GRILL

Fish and shellfish are at their best when grilled quickly over a hot fire. Above all, do not overcook these delicate foods. The best technique is simple but effective: Lightly coat a grill with oil, get it very hot, and grill the fish or seafood for only a few minutes, until just barely cooked through. A spicy herb rub or a salsa should complement, not overpower, seafood's distinctive taste.

SWORDFISH, SICILIAN STYLE

Prepare a charcoal or gas grill for direct grilling over high heat (page 107) and oil the grill rack. Coat the fish with oil.

To make the spice rub, mix together the garlic powder, basil, fennel seeds, red pepper flakes, salt, and lemon pepper in a small bowl. Sprinkle both sides of each swordfish steak generously with the spice rub.

To make the salsa, mix together the olives, tomatoes, basil, garlic, cayenne, oil, and lemon juice together in a bowl. Taste and season with salt. Set aside.

Grill the swordfish directly over high heat, turning once, until grill-marked, firm to the touch, and opaque throughout, 3–4 minutes on each side. To serve, arrange the fish steaks on individual plates and top with the salsa or serve with the salsa alongside.

Variation Tip: Serve with the salsa tossed with your favorite pasta.

MAKES 4 SERVINGS

COOKING WITH OLIVES

Wrinkled salt-cured black Sicilian olives are the perfect choice for this dish, but other salt- or brine-cured black olives would work as well. Try Greek Kalamatas, tiny black Niçoise olives, or one of the many black olives from Spain or Italy. When cooking with olives, be careful when adding salt to your dish, as most olives are themselves quite salty. Taste the olives, add them to the dish, then taste the dish to see if more salt is needed. Olives that seem too salty to begin with may be blanched for a minute in boiling water, then drained.

Olive oil for coating

4 swordfish steaks, about ½ lb (250 g) each

FOR THE SPICE RUB:

1 tablespoon garlic powder

1 tablespoon dried basil

1 teaspoon fennel seeds, ground in a mortar or spice grinder

¼ teaspoon hot red pepper flakes

1½ teaspoons salt

1 teaspoon lemon pepper or freshly ground black pepper

FOR THE SALSA:

¼ cup (1½ oz/45 g) chopped pitted Sicilian or other cured black olives

1 cup (6 oz/185 g) chopped tomatoes

¼ cup (¼ oz/7 g) chopped fresh basil

3 cloves garlic, minced

¼ teaspoon cayenne pepper

2 tablespoons extra-virgin olive oil

Juice of ½ lemon

Salt

MONKFISH SKEWERS WITH GREEN PAPAYA SLAW

Vegetable oil for coating

FOR THE SLAW:

2 cups (6 oz/185 g) peeled
and shredded green papaya

½ cup (1½ oz/45 g) thinly
sliced red onion

1 jalapeño chile

Juice of 1 lime

2 tablespoons peanut oil

1 tablespoon soy sauce

1 teaspoon Asian sesame oil

Salt

1 lb (500 g) monkfish fillets

16–20 fresh cremini or
white button mushrooms,
brushed clean

FOR THE SPICE RUB:

1 tablespoon sweet paprika

1 teaspoon *each* garlic and
onion powder

1 teaspoon Chinese
five-spice powder

1 teaspoon lemon pepper

¼ teaspoon cayenne pepper

1½ teaspoons salt

8 wooden skewers, soaked
for 30 minutes, or metal
skewers

Prepare a charcoal or gas grill for direct grilling over high heat (page 107) and oil the grill rack.

To make the slaw, combine the papaya and onion in a bowl. Seed and mince the jalapeño chile and mix into the papaya and onion along with the lime juice, peanut oil, soy sauce, and sesame oil. Taste and season with salt.

Cut the fish fillets into 1-inch (2.5-cm) chunks. Thread the chunks alternately with the whole mushrooms onto the skewers. Coat with oil.

To make the spice rub, mix together the paprika, garlic powder, onion powder, five-spice powder, lemon pepper, cayenne, and salt in a small bowl. Sprinkle generously over the skewers.

Grill the skewers directly over high heat, turning often, until the monkfish is well browned on the outside, firm to the touch, and opaque throughout, 8–10 minutes total.

Serve with the green papaya slaw.

MAKES 4 SERVINGS

GREEN PAPAYA

A papaya looks somewhat like a large pear, with thin, pale green skin that ripens to blotches of yellow and orange. In Southeast Asia and Latin America, crunchy green papaya is treated like a vegetable and appears shredded in salads. If you can find an unripe green papaya in your local market or Asian grocery, you'll enjoy the tangy flavor it gives to the Asian slaw included with this recipe. If not, use napa, savoy, or another kind of cabbage. The slaw is also good with grilled chicken.

TUNA STEAKS GRILLED OVER HERBS

Prepare a charcoal or gas grill for direct grilling over high heat (page 107) and oil the grill rack. Coat the tuna steaks with oil.

To make the rub, mix together the thyme, salt, and lemon pepper in a small bowl. Sprinkle generously on both sides of the fish.

Just before putting the fish on the grill, place the drained thyme directly on the coals or burner. Place the fish over the thyme, cover, and grill, turning once, until browned on the outside but still rare on the inside, 3–4 minutes on each side.

Serve the tuna steaks garnished with a sprig or two of thyme.

Note: Sushi-grade ahi tuna is the fish typically used by Japanese chefs for their raw tuna preparations. It is inspected more strictly for freshness and is suitable for serving rare.

Variation Tips: Use shark, swordfish, halibut, or other firm-fleshed fish steaks or fillets in place of the tuna. Lengthen the grilling time as necessary to cook these steaks or fillets until they are opaque throughout.

MAKES 4 SERVINGS

AROMATIC HERB SMOKE

Any herb with woody stalks will provide aromatic smoke and rich, intense flavor when added directly to the coals during grilling. It's a good idea to soak the herbs in water before using them so that they don't immediately catch fire. Other herbs that go well with fish and may replace the thyme in this recipe are lemon thyme, rosemary, tarragon, and oregano. Sage and rosemary are especially good with pork; oregano, marjoram, rosemary, and thyme are delicious with chicken; rosemary and thyme pair beautifully with beef; and rosemary goes well with lamb.

Olive oil or vegetable oil for coating

4 sushi-grade ahi tuna steaks, about 1 inch (2.5 cm) thick and ½ lb (250 g) each (see Note)

FOR THE HERB RUB:

1 tablespoon minced fresh thyme or 1½ teaspoons dried

2 teaspoons salt

1 teaspoon lemon pepper or freshly ground black pepper

1 or 2 bunches fresh thyme, soaked in cold water for 15 minutes and drained, plus a few sprigs for garnish

BARBECUED OYSTERS WITH GINGER-CHILE SALSA

FOR THE SALSA:

2 tablespoons peeled and minced fresh ginger

1 or 2 jalapeño or serrano chiles, seeded and minced

¼ cup (1 oz/30 g) chopped green (spring) onion, including tender green parts

1½ cups (9 oz/280 g) chopped yellow or red tomatoes

Juice of 1 lime

1 tablespoon soy sauce

1 teaspoon Asian sesame oil

Salt

48 large oysters in the shell, scrubbed

Prepare a charcoal or gas grill for direct grilling over medium-high heat (page 107).

To make the salsa, mix together the ginger, chile to taste, green onion, tomatoes, lime juice, soy sauce, and sesame oil in a bowl. Taste and season with salt.

Discard any oysters whose shells do not close to the touch. Arrange the oysters on the grill directly over medium-high heat, cover the grill, and cook the oysters until they open, 5–7 minutes. Transfer the cooked oysters to a platter and discard any that have not opened.

Using an oven mitt to protect your hand, remove the top shells. Spoon a little of the salsa onto each oyster, and serve with the remaining salsa alongside.

Serving Tip: Serve barbecued oysters as an appetizer or as a first course with Wild Mushroom Quesadillas (page 84).

MAKES 8 APPETIZER SERVINGS, 4–6 FIRST-COURSE SERVINGS

OYSTERS ON THE GRILL
The best oysters to use for barbecuing are the larger, meatier ones such as Pacific or Kumamato oysters from the West Coast. Large clams are also delicious cooked on the grill, as are scallops in the shell, if you can find them. All live bivalves, except for soft-shelled clams, should close tightly when you touch them and should open up during cooking. Discard any that don't.

SPICY SCALLOPS WITH WASABI-SAKE SAUCE

Prepare a charcoal or gas grill for direct grilling over high heat (page 107) and oil the grill rack. Have ready a special seafood grilling basket or grid if the scallops look like they might fall through the bars of the grill, or use skewers.

To make the sauce, mix together the sake, wasabi paste, ginger, and soy sauce in a small bowl. Set aside.

Lay the scallops on a platter and brush generously on both sides with sesame oil. Combine the 2 tablespoons soy sauce and wasabi, adding more soy sauce if needed to make a thin paste, and brush generously on all sides of each scallop. Let the scallops sit for 15–30 minutes before grilling.

Grill the scallops directly over high heat, turning once, until firm and opaque throughout, 3–4 minutes on all sides.

Serve the scallops with the wasabi-sake sauce for dipping.

Note: The wasabi-sake sauce is delicious with other grilled seafood or fish or with grilled chicken or pork.

Serving Tip: Serve these scallops with Grilled Red Pepper, Sweet Onion, and Tomato Salad (page 79). Make the salad before grilling the scallops.

MAKES 6 FIRST-COURSE SERVINGS, 4 MAIN-COURSE SERVINGS

WASABI

A Japanese root similar to but not related to horseradish, wasabi is widely available as a dry powder or a paste. If using the powdered form, mix it with just enough lukewarm water to give it a pasty consistency and let sit for 5–10 minutes before using. The ready-made paste comes in small tubes and has good flavor, but after opening, it can deteriorate with time. Mix prepared wasabi paste with soy sauce to make a dipping sauce for sushi or sashimi or use it in a sauce, as in this recipe.

Peanut oil or vegetable oil for coating

FOR THE WASABI-SAKE SAUCE:

½ cup (4 fl oz/125 ml) sake, mirin, or sweet sherry

1 tablespoon wasabi paste (far left)

1 tablespoon peeled and minced fresh ginger

1 tablespoon soy sauce

24 large sea scallops

Asian sesame oil for brushing

2 tablespoons soy sauce, plus more as needed

2 tablespoons wasabi paste

SOUTH-OF-THE-BORDER SEAFOOD GRILL

FOR THE TOMATO AND ONION SALAD:

4 ripe tomatoes, cut into large chunks

1 red onion, coarsely chopped

Juice of 1 lime

½ jalapeño chile, seeded and minced, or to taste

2 tablespoons olive oil

1 teaspoon salt

Vegetable oil for coating

4 small lobster tails or 8 large shrimp (prawns), peeled and deveined

8 large sea scallops

1 lb (500 g) shark, swordfish, and/or tuna fillets or steaks, cut into 1-inch (2.5-cm) chunks

1 or 2 limes

1 tablespoon pure chile powder (see Note)

2 teaspoons salt

12 large flour tortillas

4 wooden skewers, soaked for 30 minutes, or metal skewers

To make the salad, put the tomatoes in a shallow salad bowl. Add the onion and toss. In a small bowl, mix together the lime juice, chile, olive oil, and salt. Taste and adjust the seasoning. Pour the dressing over the tomatoes and onion. Let the salad sit at room temperature for up to 1 hour to allow the flavors to blend.

Prepare a charcoal or gas grill for direct grilling over high heat (page 107) and oil the grill rack.

Thread the lobster tails, scallops, and chunks of fish onto the skewers. Squeeze lime juice over the skewers. Mix the chile powder and salt together and sprinkle generously over the skewers.

Grill the seafood skewers directly over high heat, turning once, until the shellfish and fish are firm to the touch and opaque throughout, 3–5 minutes on each side. Transfer to a platter.

Grill the tortillas over high heat, turning once, until soft and lightly grill-marked, 2–3 minutes on each side.

Remove the seafood from the skewers and wrap in the tortillas. Serve with the tomato and onion salad alongside for topping the tortillas.

Note: Pure chile powder can be found in well-stocked supermarkets and Latin groceries, or purchased from mail-order sources.

MAKES 4 SERVINGS

PURE CHILE POWDER

A finely ground powder of dried chiles, pure *chile* powder should not be mistaken for the commercial spice blend known as *chili* powder. Used to season the well-known Southwestern American stew of the same name, chili powder usually combines ground dried red chiles, coriander, oregano, cumin, and often salt. It may be substituted here, but pure chile powder is preferable. The flavor of the chile variety, whether ancho, chipotle, New Mexico, or another chile, comes through in the finished dish. Experiment to see which is your favorite. If using blended chili powder, be sparing with the salt.

SALMON WITH MISO-SAKE SAUCE

Prepare a charcoal or gas grill for direct grilling over high heat (page 107) and oil the grill rack.

To make the miso-sake sauce, whisk together the sake, dashi, miso, ginger, and green onion in a saucepan over high heat. Boil until reduced by half. Remove from the heat and whisk in the cornstarch mixture. Return to low heat and cook until thickened slightly, a minute or so. Remove from the heat and keep warm.

To prepare the salmon, if using fillets, trim any skin from the fish and remove any pin bones. (If using steaks, leave the skin intact.) In a small bowl, whisk together the miso, sake, soy sauce, and wasabi. Brush both sides of the fish generously with the mixture.

Grill the salmon directly over high heat, turning once, until grill-marked, 3–4 minutes on each side. Check for doneness by cutting into the salmon at the thickest part. Salmon is good medium-rare; that is, with a center that is still deep pink or reddish. Cook longer if desired.

Spoon some sauce over the salmon and serve, passing the remaining sauce at the table.

MAKES 4 SERVINGS

MISO

Brushing fish, seafood, or chicken breasts with miso before grilling adds an appealing flavor. Miso is a fermented Japanese soybean paste that can be found in many super-markets these days, as well as in Japanese and other Asian groceries. The white and yellow varieties are milder in flavor than the red, or brown, type. Miso is also delicious whisked into the Japanese seafood broth called dashi or added to stir-fried or steamed vegetables. Base for dashi may be found in Asian groceries. Mix it with water and heat it according to the package directions to make dashi.

Vegetable oil for coating

FOR THE MISO-SAKE SAUCE:

½ cup (4 fl oz/125 ml) sake, mirin, or sweet sherry

1 cup (8 fl oz/250 ml) dashi *(far left)* or chicken or fish stock

2 tablespoons white or yellow miso *(far left)*

1 tablespoon peeled and chopped fresh ginger

¼ cup (¾ oz/20 g) chopped green (spring) onion, including tender green parts

1½ teaspoons cornstarch (cornflour) dissolved in 1 tablespoon soy sauce

FOR THE SALMON:

4 salmon steaks or fillets

½ cup (4 fl oz/125 ml) white or yellow miso

¼ cup (2 fl oz/60 ml) sake, mirin, or sweet sherry

1 tablespoon soy sauce

1 tablespoon wasabi paste

VEGETABLES ON THE GRILL

One of the best ways to cook most vegetables is on a grill. If you just rub vegetables with a little oil and toss them over the coals for a few minutes, they'll be crunchy, tender, and fresh-tasting on the plate as a side dish, in a salad, or as a vegetarian main course.

GRILLED CORN ON THE COB
WITH CHIPOTLE BUTTER

Prepare a charcoal or gas grill for direct grilling over medium-high heat (page 107) and oil the grill rack.

Coat each ear of corn with oil. Sprinkle with salt and pepper.

To make the chipotle butter, with a fork, mix together the butter with the chipotles or chile powder mixture in a small bowl. Set aside or form the butter into a log in waxed paper and refrigerate until ready to use.

Grill the corn directly over medium-high heat, turning often, until lightly grill-marked and tender yet still a bit crunchy, 5–7 minutes total. Transfer the corn to a platter, season to taste with additional salt and pepper, and top with chipotle butter before serving.

MAKES 4 SERVINGS

Vegetable oil for coating

4 ears of corn, shucked

Salt and freshly ground pepper

FOR THE CHIPOTLE BUTTER:

½ cup (4 oz/125 g) salted butter, at room temperature

2 chipotles en adobo, minced, or 1 tablespoon pure chipotle or other pure chile powder mixed with the juice of ½ lemon

GRILLING CORN

Always try to find the freshest corn available and grill it on the day you purchase it. Farmers' markets are a great source for fresh corn. You can grill corn with the husks already removed for a crunchy, lightly smoky flavor, or open up the husks, remove the silk, and rewrap the cobs in the husks for more subtle flavor and texture. Some cooks soak corn before grilling to keep it from drying out, but if the corn is fresh, this step is not necessary. Wrapping corn in aluminum foil and grilling it will steam the corn without giving it much smoky flavor.

GRILLED RED PEPPER, SWEET ONION, AND TOMATO SALAD

Olive oil or vegetable oil
for coating

2 red or yellow bell
peppers (capsicums)

2 sweet white onions
such as Maui, Vidalia, or
Walla Walla, cut into rounds
¾ inch (2 cm) thick

4 large red or yellow
tomatoes (about 2 lb/1 kg)

1 bunch fresh basil,
stemmed

FOR THE GARLIC-BALSAMIC
VINAIGRETTE:

2 cloves garlic, minced

2 tablespoons balsamic
vinegar

⅓ cup (3 fl oz/80 ml)
extra-virgin olive oil

Salt and freshly ground
pepper

Prepare a charcoal or gas grill for direct grilling over high heat (page 107) and oil the grill rack.

Put the peppers, onion rounds, and tomatoes in a bowl and coat them with oil.

Grill the peppers directly over high heat, turning to char and blister them on all sides, 5–7 minutes. Transfer to a paper bag, close the bag, and let cool for 10 minutes.

Meanwhile, grill the onion rounds, turning once, until grill-marked and partly tender, 2–3 minutes on each side. Transfer to a cutting board. Grill the tomatoes, turning often, until grill-marked, 3–4 minutes. Do not overcook. Transfer to the cutting board.

Peel the peppers and cut open to remove the seeds and stems. Chop the peppers coarsely and mound on a platter. Coarsely chop the onions and core and chop the tomatoes and add them to the platter. Scatter the basil leaves on top of the vegetables, coarsely chopping them first if desired.

To make the vinaigrette, combine the garlic and balsamic vinegar in a small bowl. Gradually whisk in the olive oil. Pour the dressing over the vegetables and toss well. Season to taste with salt and pepper and serve.

MAKES 4 SERVINGS

GRILLING PEPPERS

Peppers and chiles of all types, including ripe pimientos and mild green chiles such as Anaheims or poblanos, are delicious when grilled, and blistering their skin makes them easy to peel. If you are not grilling but want to peel peppers, you can roast them over a gas flame on the stove top or in a preheated broiler (grill) as close as possible to the heating element. Then simply follow the directions in this recipe for steaming, cooling, seeding, and peeling.

GRILLED PORTOBELLO MUSHROOMS
WITH BASIL OIL

Prepare a charcoal or gas grill for direct grilling over high heat (page 107).

Put the portobello mushroom caps on a platter and brush both sides with basil oil. Grill the caps, top side down, directly over high heat until liquid forms in the gills and the top is grill-marked, 2–4 minutes. Turn over, emptying any liquid into the fire. If flare-ups occur, move the mushrooms to a cooler part of the grill. Grill for 1–2 minutes longer, and turn again. Spoon ½ teaspoon garlic into each mushroom, along with a little more basil oil. Cook for 1–2 minutes longer.

For the last 2–3 minutes of cooking, toast the hamburger buns (if using), cut side down, on the grill over high heat. Put the mushrooms on the buns or transfer them to a plate, season with salt and pepper to taste, and serve.

Serving Tips: Grilled mushrooms make a wonderful side dish with grilled chicken (pages 10, 48) or steaks (pages 22, 26). They also serve as a delicious vegetarian entrée with a salad or Garden Skewers (page 83).

MAKES 4 SERVINGS

4 portobello mushrooms, brushed clean and stemmed

Basil oil or other flavored oil *(far left)* or olive oil for coating

2 teaspoons minced garlic

4 hamburger buns, split (optional)

Salt and freshly ground pepper

GARDEN SKEWERS

Olive oil or oil spray, or
an herb-flavored oil
(page 80)

2 zucchini (courgettes),
trimmed and cut into
1-inch (2.5-cm) chunks

12 fresh cremini or white
button mushrooms,
brushed clean

1 large red onion, cut into
1-inch (2.5-cm) chunks

1 red or yellow bell
pepper (capsicum),
seeded and cut into
1-inch (2.5-cm) chunks

Salt and freshly ground
pepper

4–6 wooden skewers,
soaked for 30 minutes,
or metal skewers

Prepare a charcoal or gas grill for direct grilling over high heat
(page 107) and oil the grill rack.

Thread the zucchini onto the skewers alternately with the whole
mushrooms, onion chunks, and pepper chunks. Coat with oil.

Grill the skewers directly over high heat, turning once, until the
vegetables are nicely grill-marked and tender-crisp, 4–6 minutes
on each side. Do not overcook; the vegetables should still be a
little crunchy.

Transfer to a platter and sprinkle with a little more oil and salt and
pepper to taste. Serve at once.

*Serving Tips: These skewers are great accompaniments for grilled
chicken, fish, seafood, or steak. The can also serve as a vegetarian
main dish, along with risotto or pasta.*

MAKES 4–6 SIDE-DISH SERVINGS, 4 MAIN-COURSE SERVINGS

GRILLING GARDEN VEGETABLES

When the garden is at its most
bountiful in midsummer, fire
up the grill for delicious, light
dinners. Almost anything you
can grow can be grilled: corn,
summer squashes, onions,
tomatoes, green beans, bell
peppers (capsicums), eggplants
(aubergines), asparagus, even
potatoes (see Grilled New
Potatoes with a Red Pepper
Crust, page 87). Brushed with
a little oil and grilled briefly
over high heat, most garden
vegetables are at their
crunchy and flavorful best.

WILD MUSHROOM QUESADILLAS

Prepare a charcoal or gas grill for direct grilling over high heat (page 107) and oil the grill rack. Grill the green chile directly over high heat, turning to char and blister it on all sides, 5–7 minutes. Transfer to a paper bag, close the bag, and let cool for 10 minutes. Peel the chile and cut open to remove the seeds and stem. Mince and set aside.

In a frying pan over medium-high heat, melt the butter. Add the mushrooms, minced chile, chile powder, and garlic, and sauté for 5–6 minutes for fresh mushrooms, 3–4 minutes for leftover grilled mushrooms. Stir in the salsa and season to taste with salt and pepper. Remove from the heat and let cool to room temperature.

Grill the tortillas on one side only until soft and lightly grill-marked, 2–3 minutes. On a work surface, lay out flat 4 sheets of aluminum foil slightly larger than the tortillas. Coat the foil with vegetable oil. Place a tortilla on each piece of foil, grilled side down, and spoon one-fourth of the mushroom mixture and one-fourth of the cheese on one half of each tortilla. Fold the tortillas over the mixture and pinch the edges together with your fingers. Do not overfill the tortillas. Fold the foil over the filled tortillas and crimp the edges to seal.

Grill the quesadilla packets directly over high heat, turning them once, 4–5 minutes on each side. Remove a packet from the grill and open the foil to take a peek. The cheese should be melted and the tortillas lightly golden and crisp. Grill 1–2 minutes longer if needed. Remove the foil and serve.

Note: For the salsa, try the Pico de Gallo on page 29.

Variation Tips: Replace the mushrooms in these quesadillas with chopped leftover Shrimp with Lemon-Garlic Butter (page 14) or chopped Grilled Chicken with Herb Rub (page 10).

MAKES 4 SERVINGS

WILD MUSHROOMS
Many varieties of exotic mushrooms are in the market these days, some gathered from the wild and others cultivated commercially. Forest-gathered mushrooms, such as chanterelles, porcini (cèpes), morels, matsutake, lobster, and others, can be found seasonally at specialty grocers and farmers' markets. Cultivated varieties, like portobello, cremini, shiitake, oyster, and enoki mushrooms, can be found in most markets year-round.

Vegetable oil for coating

1 mild green chile such as Anaheim or poblano

2 tablespoons unsalted butter

¼ lb (125 g) fresh wild mushrooms, such as porcini (cèpes), chanterelles, morels, shiitakes, or portobellos, or leftover Grilled Portobello Mushrooms with Basil Oil (page 80), finely chopped

1 tablespoon pure chile powder (page 71)

2 cloves garlic, minced

¼ cup (2 fl oz/60 ml) salsa (see Note)

Salt and freshly ground pepper

4 large flour tortillas

2 cups (8 oz/250 g) shredded Monterey jack cheese

GRILLED NEW POTATOES WITH A RED PEPPER CRUST

Olive oil for coating

24 small new potatoes

2 tablespoons sweet paprika

½ teaspoon cayenne
pepper or hot paprika,
or to taste

1 tablespoon garlic powder

1½ teaspoons salt

Prepare a charcoal or gas grill for direct cooking over medium-high heat (page 107) and oil the grill rack. If the potatoes are very small, have ready a grill basket to keep them from falling through the grill rack into the fire, or use skewers.

Parboil the potatoes in boiling water, cooking them just until they can be pierced with a knife but are not completely tender, 5–7 minutes. Do not overcook. Drain and pat dry.

Put the potatoes in a large bowl and coat with oil. In a small bowl, mix together the paprika, cayenne, garlic powder, and salt. Toss the potatoes with the spice mixture until well coated.

Grill the potatoes directly over medium-high heat, turning often, until nicely browned and tender, 10–20 minutes, depending on the size of the potatoes. Serve at once.

Preparation Tip: If you are cooking a chicken, turkey, or roast over indirect heat, you can cook these potatoes over the heated part of the grill toward the end of cooking. If grilling steaks, chops, or chicken over direct heat, small potatoes may be grilled while the meat rests.

MAKES 4 SERVINGS

POTATOES FOR GRILLING

The new potatoes called for in this recipe are small, immature waxy potatoes harvested in spring and early summer. You can choose among tiny red potatoes such as Red Bliss, tiny fingerling or banana potatoes, Yukon golds, purple or blue varieties, and a host of others. All are low in starch and have thin skins and a firm and moist texture. If you can't find new potatoes, use any small waxy potato 1–1½ inches (2.5–4 cm) in diameter. Larger potatoes may be cut into quarters or halves. Starchy russets are not a good choice for this recipe.

SOMETHING
SPECIAL

Today's grill cooks are experimenting all the time, with delicious results. Pizza acquires a wonderfully smoky flavor from grilling. Savory game can be fire-roasted or cooked on a spit to make a celebratory meal, and you can even bake chile-laced corn bread in a covered grill, or grill fresh fruit for dessert.

HERBED PIZZAS WITH
PROSCIUTTO, BASIL, AND GOAT CHEESE
90

QUAIL WITH POLENTA AND
SMOKE-GRILLED TOMATOES
93

WHOLE PORK LOIN STUFFED WITH
GREENS AND GARLIC
94

VENISON FILLET WITH WILD MUSHROOM SAUCE
97

BISTECCA ALLA FIORENTINA
98

JALAPEÑO CORN BREAD
101

GRILLED PEARS WITH
RASPBERRY–GRAND MARNIER SAUCE
102

HERBED PIZZAS WITH PROSCIUTTO, BASIL, AND GOAT CHEESE

Prepare a charcoal or gas grill for indirect cooking over high heat (400°F/200°C) (page 107) and oil the grill rack. If using a charcoal grill, arrange the coals around the perimeter to fit 2 round pizzas in the middle. For gas grills, shape the dough to fit the unheated portion of the grill or trim precooked pizza rounds as necessary.

If using homemade dough *(left),* roll each ball out on a lightly floured board into a 10-inch (25-cm) round. Whether using homemade or precooked rounds, brush both sides with olive oil and sprinkle with a little cornmeal.

Place the rounds on the unheated portion of the grill. (If your grill has a widely spaced grid, you may need to use a grill basket for homemade dough.) Cook, turning once, until grill-marked and cooked or heated through, 5–8 minutes on each side for uncooked pizza rounds, 3–4 minutes on each side for precooked rounds. Transfer to a work surface.

Grill the bell peppers directly over high heat, turning to char and blister them on all sides, 5–7 minutes. Transfer to a paper bag, close the bag, and let cool for 10 minutes. Peel and cut open the peppers to remove the seeds and stems. Chop and set aside.

Spread half of the tomato sauce on each pizza round. Top each round with half of the bell peppers and half of the prosciutto. Dot each pizza with half of the goat cheese and sprinkle with half of the basil. Sprinkle with salt and pepper to taste and drizzle a little olive oil on top.

Place the pizzas on the unheated part of the grill, cover the grill, and bake over indirect high heat until the topping is thoroughly heated through, about 10 minutes. Serve immediately.

MAKES 4 SERVINGS

HERBED PIZZA DOUGH

Mix 1 package (1½ teaspoons) active dry yeast with ¾ cup (6 fl oz/180 ml) warm water and 1 teaspoon sugar and let sit for a few minutes, until foamy. Combine 2 cups (10 oz/315 g) all-purpose (plain) flour, ¼ cup (2 fl oz/60 ml) olive oil, 2 tablespoons dried basil, and ½ teaspoon salt in a bowl. Stir in the yeast mixture. Knead on a lightly floured board until smooth and elastic, 10 minutes. Place in an oiled bowl, turn, cover, and let rise in a warm place until doubled in size, 1–2 hours. Divide in half and form into 2 balls. Use as directed *(right).*

Herbed Pizza Dough *(far left)* or precooked pizza rounds 10 inches (25 cm) in diameter

Olive oil for coating

Cornmeal for sprinkling

2 red or yellow bell peppers (capsicums)

1 cup (8 fl oz/250 ml) tomato sauce (page 33 or your favorite)

¼ lb (125 g) sliced prosciutto, cut into fine shreds

¼ lb (125 g) fresh goat cheese

2 tablespoons chopped fresh basil or 1 tablespoon dried

Salt and freshly ground pepper

QUAIL WITH POLENTA AND SMOKE-GRILLED TOMATOES

Olive oil for coating

4 strips bacon or pancetta

4 quail, preferably partially boned by the butcher, leaving leg bones intact

FOR THE HERB PASTE:

2 tablespoons minced fresh tarragon or 1 table-spoon dried

4 cloves garlic, minced

1½ teaspoons salt

1 teaspoon freshly ground pepper

1 teaspoon olive oil

1 cup (7 oz/220 g) polenta, cooked, cooled, and cut into squares (far right)

8 large tomatoes, about 4 lb (2 kg) total weight

2 cloves garlic, minced

2 teaspoons chopped fresh tarragon or 1 teaspoon dried

Salt and freshly ground pepper

Wood chips or chunks, soaked for 30 minutes and drained (page 111)

Prepare a charcoal or gas grill for indirect grilling over medium-high heat (page 107) and oil the grill rack. With kitchen string, tie a strip of bacon around the breast of each quail and tie the legs together.

To make the herb paste, mix together the tarragon, garlic, salt, pepper, and olive oil. Rub the paste all over the quail.

Sprinkle the wood chips on the coals, or add in a perforated foil packet to a gas grill (page 111). Grill the quail directly over medium-high heat, turning often, until well browned, 5–7 minutes. Move them to the unheated part of the grill, cover the grill, and cook. After 15 minutes, check for doneness by cutting into a quail at the inside of the thigh or testing with an instant-read thermometer. The quail are done when they no longer show any pink and read at least 160°F (71°C). Continue cooking for up to 15 minutes more, as needed. Transfer to a platter and cover loosely with foil.

Grill the polenta squares over direct heat, turning once, until nicely golden and heated through, 4–5 minutes on each side. Transfer to a platter. At the same time, grill the tomatoes over direct heat, turning often, until grill-marked and beginning to soften, 5–7 minutes total. Do not overcook. Transfer the tomatoes to a cutting board and core and chop them coarsely. Transfer to a bowl, stir in the garlic and tarragon, and season to taste with salt and pepper.

Remove the string from each quail breast and, if desired, the legs. Serve on a bed of grilled polenta and chopped tomatoes.

MAKES 4 SERVINGS

GRILLING POLENTA

Polenta, coarsely ground cornmeal, is perfect for grilling once it has been cooked, cooled, and sliced. To cook, whisk the polenta into 3 cups boiling water and stir constantly over low heat, 10–15 minutes for a soft texture. Next, pour the soft polenta out onto a lightly greased baking pan to a depth of 1½ inches (4 cm). After about 2 hours, cut the cooled polenta into four 4-inch (10-cm) squares and proceed with the recipe.

WHOLE PORK LOIN STUFFED WITH GREENS AND GARLIC

PORK LOIN

The loin, or the upper back section of the pig between the shoulder and the leg, is the most tender cut of pork. The long, thin pork center loin is often sliced into boneless chops. In this recipe, the whole center loin is cut crosswise into 2 equal pieces, which are laid together, stuffed, and tied with kitchen string to make a thicker, more compact roast.

Prepare a charcoal or gas grill for indirect grilling over medium-high heat, setting a drip pan under the unheated part of the grill (page 107). This is a good dish to cook on a spit, if you have a rotisserie setup for your grill (page 111).

Put the chard with its rinsing water still clinging to it in a large frying pan, cover, and steam until wilted, 3–4 minutes. Uncover, add the olive oil, two-thirds of the garlic, and salt and pepper to taste. Cook for 3–4 minutes longer, stirring often. Remove from the heat and let cool. Squeeze gently to remove excess liquid.

Place the pork loin halves on a work surface, fat side down. Sprinkle the top side with salt and pepper. Arrange the chopped chard down the center of one piece and cover with the other, fat side up. Tie in 4 or 5 places with kitchen string to make a cylindrical roast. Rub the outside of the roast with the remaining garlic. Rub with salt, pepper, and sage.

Sprinkle the wood chips on the coals, or add in a perforated foil packet to a gas grill (page 111). Arrange the roast in the center of the grill over the drip pan, or place it on a rotisserie spit. Cover the grill and cook, maintaining the heat at medium-high, for 1 hour, adding more coals as needed. Check for doneness by cutting into the center of the roast or testing with an instant-read thermometer. The pork should be slightly pink at the center and still juicy, or 155°F (68°C). Continue cooking as needed. Transfer to a platter, loosely cover with aluminum foil, and let rest for 10 minutes. Cut into slices and serve.

Serving Tip: Serve pork with Grilled Red Pepper, Sweet Onion, and Tomato Salad (page 79). Grill the vegetables over direct heat while the pork cooks over indirect heat or rests before serving.

MAKES 8–10 SERVINGS

4 cups (8 oz/250 g) chopped Swiss chard

2 tablespoons olive oil

6 cloves garlic, minced

Salt and freshly ground pepper

1 boneless pork loin roast, about 7 lb (3.5 kg), cut crosswise into 2 equal pieces and trimmed of fat

2 tablespoons minced fresh sage or 1 tablespoon dried

Wood chips or chunks, soaked for 30 minutes and drained (page 111)

VENISON FILLET WITH WILD MUSHROOM SAUCE

Olive oil or vegetable oil for coating

4 slices bacon or pancetta

1 venison fillet, 3–4 lb (1.5–2 kg), trimmed

Salt and ground pepper

1 tablespoon chopped fresh rosemary

2 cloves garlic, minced

FOR THE SAUCE:

2 tablespoons unsalted butter

1 lb (500 g) wild mushrooms such as shiitakes, porcini, or portobellos, brushed clean and coarsely chopped

¼ cup (1 oz/30 g) minced shallot

3 cloves garlic, minced

1 teaspoon minced fresh rosemary

1 teaspoon minced fresh thyme

2 cups (16 fl oz/500 ml) beef stock or canned low-sodium beef broth

Salt and ground pepper

1 tablespoon cornstarch (cornflour) dissolved in 2 tablespoons sweet sherry or port

Prepare a charcoal or gas grill for direct grilling over medium-high heat (page 107) and oil the grill rack.

Arrange the bacon slices lengthwise on top of the fillet and tie in 2 or 3 places with kitchen string. Rub the fillet all over with oil, then sprinkle with salt and pepper. (Since bacon is salty, use a light hand with the salt.) Rub the rosemary and garlic all over the fillet.

Grill the fillet directly over medium-high heat, turning the meat occasionally, for a total of 10–14 minutes. (Move the fillet to an unheated portion of the grill if flare-ups occur.) Check the meat for doneness by cutting into the center or testing with an instant-read thermometer. Rare will be quite red at the center and should read 120–125°F (49°–52°C); medium-rare will be red to pink and 130–135°F (54°–57°C). Due to its leanness, most game meat should be cooked only to medium-rare; longer cooking will result in dry and tough meat. Transfer to a platter, loosely cover with aluminum foil, and let rest for 10 minutes.

Meanwhile, make the sauce. In a saucepan over medium-high heat, melt the butter and add the mushrooms, shallot, garlic, rosemary, and thyme. Sauté until soft, 4–5 minutes. Add the stock, increase the heat to high, and cook until reduced by half, about 5 minutes. Season to taste with salt and pepper. Remove the sauce from the heat. Stir in the cornstarch mixture and cook over medium heat until thickened, about 1 minute.

Slice the meat against the grain on the diagonal and serve with the wild mushroom sauce.

Variation Tips: Replace the venison with beef fillet, omitting the bacon, if you like. If using beef, you can cook it until medium, or pink in the center and 140°F (60°C). The wild mushroom sauce is also good with grilled or roast chicken.

MAKES 6–8 SERVINGS

BARDING

Farm-raised game meats and birds, such as venison, ostrich, quail, and squab, are good choices for the grill. Game is naturally lean, so barding, or wrapping the meat or poultry in bacon or pancetta, compensates for its lack of fat and helps to keep the meat juicy and flavorful. Bacon will provide a lightly smoked flavor, while pancetta is unsmoked. You can also use thinly sliced pork fatback (uncured fat cut from the back of the pig) for barding.

BISTECCA ALLA FIORENTINA

If using dried beans, put the beans in a pot and add water to cover. Bring to a boil over high heat, turn off the burner, and cover the pot. Let the beans soak for 1 hour. Drain off the water and add fresh water to cover. Bring to a boil, reduce the heat to a simmer. Cover and cook until tender, about 2 hours. In a large bowl, combine the cooked or canned beans with the oregano, onion, minced garlic, olive oil, parsley, lemon juice, and salt and pepper to taste. Set aside and let cool to room temperature.

Prepare a charcoal or gas grill for direct cooking over medium-high heat (page 107) and oil the grill rack.

Rub the steaks all over with olive oil. Rub the cut sides of the garlic halves all over the steaks. Sprinkle the steaks generously with salt and pepper on both sides.

Sprinkle the wood chips on the coals, or add in a perforated foil packet to a gas grill (page 111). Grill the steaks directly over medium-high heat, turning occasionally and moving to a cooler part of the grill if flare-ups occur, 10–12 minutes total. Cut into the center of a steak near the bone or test with an instant-read thermometer. Rare steaks will be quite red near the bone and should read 120°–125°F (49°–52°C); medium-rare will be red to pink and read 130°–135°F (54°–57°C); medium will be pink and read 140°F (60°C). Transfer to a platter, loosely cover with aluminum foil, and let rest for 10 minutes.

Serve the steak with the spinach and room-temperature beans.

Serving Tip: Porterhouse steaks are composed of the fillet and the strip loin. To serve, carve each steak into fillet pieces and loin pieces. Slice each thickly and give each diner pieces of both. If porterhouse steaks are not available, T-bone steaks can also be used.

MAKES 4 SERVINGS

SAUTÉED SPINACH

In Florence, this grilled steak is often served with white beans and a side of sautéed spinach. For the spinach, heat 2 tablespoons extra-virgin olive oil in a saucepan over medium heat and sauté 2 cloves thinly sliced garlic until lightly golden, 3–4 minutes. Do not let it burn.

Add 1 lb (500 g) stemmed spinach, with its rinsing water still clinging to it, and the juice of 1 lemon, cover, and cook, stirring occasionally, until the spinach wilts, 4–5 minutes. Do not overcook. Season to taste with salt and pepper.

FOR THE CANNELLINI BEANS:

1 lb (500 g) dried or 2 cups (14 oz/440 g) canned cannellini or other white beans

1 tablespoon minced fresh oregano or 1½ teaspoons dried

¼ cup (1 oz/30 g) finely chopped yellow onion

1 clove garlic, minced

¼ cup (2 fl oz/60 ml) extra-virgin olive oil

2 tablespoons minced fresh flat-leaf (Italian) parsley

Juice of 1 lemon

Salt and freshly ground pepper

Olive oil for coating

2 porterhouse steaks, 2 inches (5 cm) thick

4 cloves garlic, halved

Salt and freshly ground pepper

Sautéed Spinach *(far left)* for serving

Wood chips or chunks, soaked for 30 minutes and drained (page 111)

JALAPEÑO CORN BREAD

1 cup (5 oz/155 g) yellow cornmeal

1 cup (5 oz/155 g) all-purpose (plain) flour

2 tablespoons sugar

1 tablespoon baking powder

1 teaspoon salt

⅓ cup (3 fl oz/80 ml) corn oil, plus more for coating

1 cup (8 fl oz/250 ml) low-fat milk

1 egg

½–1 jalapeño chile, seeded and minced

¼ cup (1 oz/30 g) finely chopped yellow onion

Prepare a charcoal or gas grill for indirect cooking over high heat (400°F/200°C)(page 107). Oil an 8-inch (20-cm) square or a 6-by-9-inch (15-by-23-cm) baking pan or a 10-inch (25-cm) cast-iron frying pan.

In a large bowl, mix together the cornmeal, flour, sugar, baking powder, and salt. In another bowl, beat the ⅓ cup oil, milk, and egg together. Stir the wet ingredients into the dry ingredients. Stir in jalapeño to taste and the onion. Spoon the batter into the prepared pan.

Place a sturdy heatproof metal cake rack on the grill over the unheated portion and put the pan on the rack (see Note). Cover the grill and bake until a skewer inserted into the center of the corn bread comes out clean, about 25 minutes. Serve while still warm or cooled to room temperature.

Note: Placing the corn bread on a metal cake rack on the grill will help keep the bottom from browning too quickly.

MAKES 8 SERVINGS

BAKING ON THE GRILL
A grill prepared for indirect cooking and covered acts as an oven and can be used to bake anything from corn bread to fruit cobbler to deep-dish chicken pie. It's handy to have a grill already equipped with a built-in thermometer, since you want to maintain an even temperature throughout the baking process. But you can also check the temperature by setting an oven thermometer inside a covered kettle grill or inserting an instant-read thermometer into one of the cover's top vents. Aluminum foil drip pans that are 6 by 9 by 1½ inches (15 by 23 by 4 cm) are handy pans for baking.

GRILLED PEARS WITH
RASPBERRY–GRAND MARNIER SAUCE

GRILLING FRUIT

Fruits of all kinds can be successfully grilled, making dramatic and unusual desserts. Use firm fruit, as softer fruit can quickly turn mushy. Winter pears are excellent, as are peaches and nectarines. Pineapple slices and whole bananas can also be grilled, although care should be taken not to overcook them. Ice cream, mascarpone, and fruit sauce are all wonderful to serve alongside grilled fruit.

Prepare a charcoal or gas grill for direct grilling over medium-high heat (page 107) and oil the grill rack.

To make the sauce, combine the raspberries and honey in a bowl. Mash the raspberries lightly with a fork and stir in the liqueur. Set aside.

Cut the pears in half lengthwise and remove the cores. Squeeze the lemon over the cut sides of the pears to prevent browning. In a shallow bowl, stir together the sugar and cinnamon. Dip the cut sides of the pears in the cinnamon sugar.

Grill the pears, cut side down, directly over medium-high heat until the fruit is grill-marked and the sugar is caramelized, 2–4 minutes. Do not allow to char. Using a spatula, turn the pears and grill until tender and heated through, 3–4 minutes. If the pears start to char, move them to a cooler part of the grill to cook.

Serve the pears topped with the raspberry sauce and with a scoop of vanilla ice cream alongside, if desired.

Serving Tip: Serve the grilled pears with a small glass of pear eau-de-vie, a clear fruit brandy. You could also use the eau-de-vie in the sauce in place of the orange liqueur, if you wish, and increase the honey to taste.

MAKES 4 SERVINGS

Vegetable oil for coating

FOR THE SAUCE:

1 cup (4 oz/125 g) fresh or thawed frozen raspberries

1 teaspoon honey

1 tablespoon Grand Marnier or other orange-flavored liqueur

4 Bosc, Anjou, or other firm winter pears

1 lemon, halved crosswise

¾ cup (6 oz/185 g) sugar

1 tablespoon ground cinnamon

Vanilla ice cream for serving (optional)

FUELING THE FIRE

The outdoor cook faces an array of choices when it comes to fuels. Some knowledge of the different properties of different fuels will help you make the right selection for your grill and for the food you're cooking.

FOR GAS GRILLS

For most gas grills, propane is the fuel of choice. You can find already-filled tanks of this clean-burning gas in hardware stores and specialty grill stores. One tank will last for many hours of cooking, but it's always a good idea to keep a spare tank on hand. Color-coded magnetic patches attached to the side of the tank will clearly display the fuel's level. Look for dealers who will refill empty tanks or exchange filled ones for empty ones at a reasonable price. When propane tanks are not in use, store them away from direct sunlight, but keep them out of garages or other enclosed storage areas. Read and follow all precautions printed on the tank.

It is also possible to hook up a gas grill to a natural-gas line in your patio. Be aware that gas grills need to be adapted mechanically to burn that type of fuel efficiently and provide adequate cooking heat. Have a professional from a specialty grill store do the hookup and adaptation for you.

FOR CHARCOAL GRILLS

The most readily available fuel choice for a charcoal grill is charcoal briquettes. These compact, uniform, square pillow-shaped lumps of fuel are made by compressing pulverized charcoal with binding agents, such as sawdust, and additives that facilitate lighting and burning. They make a good fire, are easy to use, and provide steady, spark-free heat. But the binding agents they include can leave an unpleasant aftertaste in food. Avoid briquettes containing nitrates, petroleum, sand, or clay as fillers and always avoid self-igniting briquettes, which may violate air-quality control standards in some areas. Store all types of briquettes in a dry place.

Hardwood charcoal, on the other hand, makes a hot, cleaner-burning fire. These lumps of fragrant hardwood—mesquite is the most common, but you can often find hickory, alder, oak, apple, pecan, or cherry—have already been burned until they are charred to almost pure carbon. Break large chunks of hardwood charcoal into smaller, more uniform pieces before lighting the fire, to ensure that the charcoal heats evenly. Keep a careful eye on the fire, as the charcoal will throw off some sparks at first. Like briquettes, hardwood charcoal should be stored in a dry place.

PREPARING THE GRILL

The most important thing to keep in mind about preparing a fire for outdoor cooking is to allow yourself enough time for the fire to get hot.

If you are using a charcoal grill, the coals need 20 to 30 minutes from the time you light them until they are ready for cooking. You can tell at a glance when they are sufficiently hot: they will be evenly covered in light gray ash or, at night, they will glow red. Gas grills require lighting 10 to 15 minutes in advance, so that their lava-rock or ceramic-briquette beds or metal baffles have time to heat up fully.

STARTING A GAS GRILL

For cooks using a gas grill, starting the fire is a simple matter. First, open the grill lid and make sure that the burner controls are turned off. If you are using fuel from a propane tank, make sure the tank has fuel in it. Then simply turn on the valve. Light the grill following the manufacturer's instructions. If your gas grill does not have an automatic spark-inducing ignition button, use long wooden fireplace matches to ignite the gas jets. Turn the knobs to adjust the heat level; then close the lid and let the bed of lava rock, ceramic briquettes, or metal baffles heat for 10 to 15 minutes.

STARTING A CHARCOAL FIRE

To avoid unpleasant fumes that can permeate food, and to limit your contribution to air pollution, do not use starter fluid or charcoal that has been presaturated with starter fluid. A proper arrangement of coals makes starter fluid unnecessary and ensures quick, even burning of the coals.

The most basic method calls for laying a base of paraffin-saturated corn cobs or similar fuel-soaked starting aids in the fire bed at the bottom of the grill. Alternatively, if an electrical outlet is close by, position the coil of an electric fire starter in the fire bed. On top of the starting aid(s), arrange a compact pyramid of charcoal pieces, using enough coals to eventually cover the bottom of the grill in an even bed, for direct grilling, or to arrange coals around a drip pan, for indirect grilling. Then, use a match to ignite the starting aids, or plug in the electric starter.

Alternatively, try a chimney starter, which is a metal cylinder with vents and a handle. Put the chimney starter on the fire bed. Stuff crumpled newspaper into the bottom of the chimney and pile the charcoal on top. Center the chimney in the grill and light the paper. The flames burning upward inside the chimney will ignite the coals.

Whichever method you use, the coals should be ready in about 20 minutes. Once the coals are ready, they must be spread in the fire pan as required by the cooking method (see below). Use long metal tongs with a heatproof handle to spread the coals as desired in the grill's fire bed.

DIRECT AND INDIRECT GRILLING

Before you begin cooking, determine whether you'll need direct or indirect heat. Foods grilled over direct heat are placed directly over hot coals or the burners of a gas grill. This intense, high-heat method is used for searing and for grilling small or thin food items that take less than 25 minutes to cook, including some poultry pieces, steaks, chops, hamburgers, sausages, fish fillets, and kabobs.

For a direct-heat fire in a gas grill, heat all the burners beneath the rack on which you plan to cook to medium-high or high. To set up a direct-heat fire in a charcoal grill, use long-handled metal tongs or another long tool to spread hot coals evenly across the area of the fire bed directly below where the food will sit.

Indirect heat, on the other hand, cooks foods by reflected heat, much like roasting in an oven. Use this method for grilling larger pieces of food such as a boned leg of lamb or a whole chicken. Heat circulating inside the grill cooks the food more slowly and evenly, although you may turn the food partway through the cooking time to ensure uniform cooking. Indirect-heat cooking requires that the grill be kept covered. Every time you lift the lid, heat escapes, which can increase the cooking time.

For an indirect-heat fire in a gas grill, first preheat the grill using all the burners, then turn off the burners directly beneath where the food will sit and place a drip pan below the rack (an aluminum-foil roasting pan is ideal). Replace the grill rack, put the food over the drip pan, and adjust the burners on either side of the food to provide equal amounts of heat.

To set up an indirect-heat fire in a charcoal grill, center the drip pan on the fire bed and use a pair of long-handled tongs to position the hot coals along the edges of the pan. This will prevent any drippings from the food from falling into the fire and causing flare-ups. Arrange the coals on both sides of the drip pan or around its perimeter. Put the food on the center of the grill rack directly over the pan and cover the grill.

For foods that require 40 minutes or more of indirect cooking time, light a second batch of coals in

PREVENTING FLARE-UPS

When dripping fat causes flames to flare up during grilling, some cooks control the flames by dousing them with water from a spray bottle. Bear in mind, however, that steam from flames sprayed too close to you can cause burns, plus cold water can crack the finish of a hot grill. A better method of halting flare-ups is simply to move the food to a cooler part of the grill and, if needed, to cover the grill and close its vents.

PREPARING FOOD FOR GRILLING

One of the keys to successful grilling is adding flavor to food by seasoning it before cooking. Old grilling recipes told cooks not to add salt to meat before cooking, or it would dry out. Actually, salt, pepper, herbs, and other seasonings not only add flavor to grilled foods but also form a savory, caramelized crust that keeps meat, poultry, and fish juicy and tender.

Fish should be trimmed of excess skin, and any small bones remaining in fillets should be removed with needle-nose pliers. Most vegetables don't need to be peeled before grilling; just cut them into shapes and sizes convenient for the grill.

Prior to cooking meat, trim off most of the external fat and discard it.

Internal fat or marbling promotes tenderness and flavor, but external fat causes flare-ups as it melts and drips into the fire. Remove external fat from poultry for the same reason. Some cooks skin chicken before grilling to cut down on fat, but skin protects delicate meat, keeping it from drying out, and adds flavor during cooking. Better to keep the skin on during cooking and remove it afterward, if desired.

Very thick cuts of meat, such as leg of lamb or a large beef tenderloin, should be boned (if applicable) and butterflied before grilling. This may be done by the butcher, but all it requires is a boning knife and some practice. In the case of leg of lamb, bone the leg by cutting lengthwise along the leg and hip bones and pulling the meat away, keeping the meat in one piece. Remove the bones. Spread the boneless meat out on a cutting board, cut side up. It will be unevenly thick, and you want to even it out. Holding the knife parallel to the cutting board, cut into the thicker part of the meat, opening it up like a book as you cut and laying it flat until you have one evenly thick piece of meat. You can stabilize the wide, flat piece of meat, making it easier to turn on the grill, by inserting long skewers lengthwise into the meat.

OILING THE GRILL

Oiling the grill is essential when cooking fish and seafood, most vegetables, and nonfatty meats and poultry. Use vegetable oil on a paper towel to oil the grill, or try one of the many oil sprays available in the supermarket. (Use the spray to oil the grill before the coals or burners are lit; it is quite dangerous to spray oil at a fire.) It's generally a good idea to oil the food as well before grilling it. You can rub or brush on oil or use oil spray. Salt, pepper, herbs, or spices or a spice rub can be sprinkled or rubbed on after coating with oil and will stick to the food better. Fattier cuts of meat (pork shoulder, spareribs) need not be oiled before grilling.

ADDING FLAVOR WITH SMOKE

Cooking on a grill itself contributes some flavor in the form of smoke that rises from small flare-ups caused by fat and juices dripping into the fire. More flavor still can be added through the smoke from aromatic wood chips or chunks, as well as from dried herbs scattered loose over the coals or placed in a smoker box on a gas grill.

Choose aromatic additions to complement food as you would choose spices or herbs. Mesquite, hickory, alder, apple, and pecan woods deliver wisps of rich, sweet flavor. Woody herbs such as rosemary, oregano, thyme, and dried basil stems also contribute their familiar flavors, whether they are used on their own or blended. Such herbs may sometimes be found packaged in bags that resemble tea bags, for a mess-free addition to a fire. Consider, too, using large, sturdy rosemary twigs as skewers for kabobs.

Before use, soak wood chips, chunks, or herbs in water for 30 minutes, then drain them well. If using a charcoal grill, add them directly to the coals while the food cooks, timing the addition so the flavor of the smoke they generate enhances but does not dominate whatever you are cooking. Robust meats, for example, can take longer smoking, while just a few minutes of smoke toward the end of cooking is enough for mild seafood.

To use wood chips or herbs with a gas grill, look for a small, vented metal smoker box into which the soaked aromatics may be put for placing directly over burners. The box will prevent small particles from clogging the fuel ports. You can also make a small packet of chips or herbs using heavy-duty aluminum foil. Fold the foil around a handful of chips or herbs and perforate the top of the packet with a fork or the tip of a knife. Place the packet directly on the ceramic bricks, lava rocks, or metal baffles above the burners. If you are cooking a roast or whole bird that requires considerable time in a covered grill, replenish wood in the smoker box or add newly made up packets as needed.

ROTISSERIE GRILLS

Whether it comes built into your gas or charcoal grill or is available as an attachable accessory, a rotisserie consists of a large spit positioned above the fire bed, slowly rotated at a constant speed by an electric motor. Evenly balanced on the spit and held securely in place with adjustable pronged forks that clamp firmly to the spit, a large meat roast or whole bird will cook slowly and evenly on a rotisserie. Look for sturdy models with strong, reliable motors.

The key to using a rotisserie is to balance food as evenly as possible on the spit. If the food is not well balanced, the motor will strain and jerk, resulting in uneven cooking, lost juices, and undue stress on the motor. Most rotisseries come with a counter-weight system, which can be adjusted to compensate for the awkward shape of certain food items. It is preferable to have two people on hand for ease when mounting any food item onto a rotisserie spit. Use sturdy linen kitchen string to truss whole poultry and to tie roasts into more compact shapes. Prepare the fire for indirect-heat cooking (page 107), positioning a drip pan directly beneath the food to prevent flare-ups. The food will baste itself as it turns, but, if you like, you can also baste it using drippings from the pan.

Recipes in this book that are suitable for spit-roasting are Whole Grill-Roasted Turkey (page 55), Quail with Polenta and Smoke-Grilled Tomatoes (page 93), Whole Pork Loin Stuffed with Greens and Garlic (page 94), Venison Fillet with Wild Mushroom Sauce (page 97), and, if the boned lamb leg is rolled and tied, Butterflied Leg of Lamb with Rosemary-Garlic Paste (page 17).

CHECKING FOR DONENESS

The variable intensity of a grill's heat and the simple change of scene from kitchen to backyard can sometimes cause uncertainty over how long some foods need to cook to the desired degree of doneness. Always bear in mind that times will vary with the particular type of grill and fuel you use and the size, thickness, and temperature of the particular ingredients you have chosen. In most of the recipes in this book, times are provided in a range of 5 or 10 minutes as an estimate of when foods might be done. These are guidelines and should not be taken to mean that the food will be done in exactly this number of minutes. Use an instant-read meat thermometer to check the food and follow the temperatures recommended. If you don't have a thermometer, cut into the food and check the interior visually, following the cues provided in the recipes.

MEAT

To judge the doneness of meat cooked on a grill visually, cut into the thickest part. Rare meat will look reddish in the center, medium-rare will be rosy pink in the center, and medium will have just a trace of pink. Cooking meat beyond medium may cause it to dry out and become tough. (Hamburgers are an exception; for safety's sake, they should be cooked no less than medium, and many health experts say it is wiser to cook them to at least medium-well or 160°F/71°C.) If using an instant-read thermometer inserted into the thickest part of a piece of meat away from the bone, look for 120° to 125°F (49° to 52°C) for rare meat, 130°F (54°C) for medium-rare, and 140°F (60°C) for medium. Pork should be cooked to 155° to 160°F (68° to 71°C).

All meat should rest before serving for 5 to 15 minutes, depending on the size and thickness of the cut, and tented with aluminum foil. This allows the juices to redistribute and ensures juiciness and flavor. The internal temperature will go up 5° to 10°F (2° to 4°C) as the meat sits.

POULTRY

Grilling poultry is best done using a combination of direct and indirect grilling to make sure all the pieces are thoroughly cooked. Chicken and turkey are done when they are opaque throughout, with no trace of pink remaining when cut into at the bone or at the center of boneless pieces. When pieces are pierced with a long-handled fork, the juices should run clear. For safety's sake, all chicken should register at least 160°F (71°C) when an instant-read thermometer is inserted in the thickest part, away from the bone. Cooking times will vary depending on the thickness of the pieces and whether they are boned and/or skinless. Chicken quarters will take the most time, and boneless, skinless chicken breasts the least.

SEAFOOD

In general, fish should be cooked until it flakes when a knife is inserted into the flesh. Count on an average of 5 to 8 minutes per inch (2.5 cm) of thickness. Shrimp (prawns) should be cooked until uniformly opaque throughout. Clams, mussels, and oysters should be well scrubbed before cooking. Discard any that are not tightly closed. They should be cooked just until their shells open. Discard any that do not open. Do not overcook fish or seafood. Cut into a piece to check doneness. Some fish, such as salmon and tuna, are best served rare to raw on the inside.

VEGETABLES

Grilling is an excellent way to cook most vegetables. The trick is to avoid overcooking them, making vegetables just tender enough to eat while keeping them fresh and crunchy. The only way to tell is to taste, so pick up that asparagus or zucchini or ear of corn after you've had it on the grill for a few minutes and take a bite. Coat the vegetables with oil before cooking, using a flavored oil if you have one (page 115).

GRILLING SAFETY

Whenever you grill, remember the following important safety points:

Never spray starter fluid, oil, or another flammable liquid on already-lit charcoal.

From the moment you ignite the coals to the moment you dispose of the cooled ashes, never leave your grill unwatched or unattended.

Always keep children and pets safely away from the grill.

Do not wear loose clothing when grilling, and tie back long hair.

Always use your grill out in the open on a level surface, well clear of enclosures, overhangs, or anything combustible such as dry grass.

Use only fire starters specifically designed for grill use and store them in a safe, secure place away from the grill. Other fuels, such as kerosene or gasoline, should also not be placed anywhere near an outdoor grill.

Do not use chimney or electric-coil starters with instant-lighting briquettes.

If using an electric-coil starter, as soon as the coals are lit, unplug it and place it on a fireproof surface until it cools completely.

Keep a water hose and/or fire extinguisher ready in case of fire.

FOOD SAFETY

Grilling goes hand in hand with warm summer weather—and so does food poisoning. But the risk is present all year round. To guard against food-borne illness, keep the following guidelines in mind:

If the food you plan to cook is frozen, defrost it completely in the refrigerator or microwave, not at room temperature. Uncooked food should never sit out for more than 2 hours, or 1 hour during hot weather.

Check sell-by and use-by dates on packaging. Throw out anything that looks or smells in any way suspicious.

Always wash your hands with plenty of warm, soapy water, especially before and after handling raw meat, poultry, or seafood.

Do not return cooked food to the unwashed platters or plates on which they sat when raw. If basting with a marinade in which raw food sat, bring the liquid to a boil in a saucepan before using, or stop using the basting liquid at least 5 minutes before finishing cooking. Wash brushes that were used on raw food before using them on cooked food.

Follow suggested internal temperatures to make sure food is cooked long enough to kill any bacteria.

Refrigerate leftovers promptly. Food should not sit out for longer than 2 hours at most, or 1 hour during hot weather.

CARING FOR THE GRILL

Grills are low-maintenance tools but do require some attention. With a little regular care, many grills will cook efficiently and cleanly for many years.

Before you begin to cook, brush or spray the rack or grid with oil to help keep food from sticking and to make cleanup easier.

While the grill is still hot after cooking, use a long-handled wire brush to scrape off any food particles stuck to the rack. Cover the grill and allow the heat of the dying coals or gas flames to burn off the residue.

Don't let ashes accumulate in a charcoal grill. Clean out the fire pan frequently. Wait until the ash is completely cool, scoop it out, and discard it in a nonflammable container.

After a gas grill has completely cooled, sort through its lava rocks or ceramic briquettes, dislodging and removing any bits of food that could clog the gas jets. Replace the rocks or briquettes if they are heavily soiled and no longer heat efficiently. Do not wash the rocks with detergent. Clean metal baffles occasionally by scraping off accumulated grease and ash.

Never line the fire bed or cooking rack with any material. Grills get very hot, and any foreign substance presents a risk of catching fire. Lining a grill with aluminum foil can hinder the necessary flow of air.

Protect your grill with a waterproof cover or store it indoors.

GLOSSARY

ASIAN CHILE OIL/SAUCE Asian chile oils and sauces come in many colors, flavors, and heat levels. Indonesian *sambal oelek* and *sambal badjak* are among the hottest. Chinese chile oil and sauce add both heat and flavor to marinades and stir-fries. *Sriracha,* a bright red, hot chile sauce from Thailand, delivers zest to many Southeast Asian dishes. Thai sweet chile sauce, a blend of sugar, water, and red chiles, is delicious on fish, seafood, and chicken. Look for these oils and sauces in well-stocked supermarkets and Asian groceries.

CAYENNE PEPPER A very hot red pepper made from ground dried cayenne and other chiles, cayenne is used sparingly to add heat or to heighten flavor. Because different blends vary in heat, and because only a little is needed, always begin with a very small amount and add more to taste in small pinches.

CHILES, ROASTING AND PEELING Roasting mild green chiles or bell peppers (capsicums) makes them easy to peel and brings out their flavor. Roast them over the grill or on a gas burner, turning occasionally, until the skin is blistered. Place in a paper bag and let cool. Peel off the skin and cut open to remove the stems and seeds.

CHINESE FIVE-SPICE POWDER Five-spice powder is a common seasoning in the kitchens of southern China and of Vietnam, where it is often used to flavor poultry for roasting. Although it is readily available in well-stocked food stores, making your own results in a more flavorful blend. Using a coffee grinder or mortar and pestle, grind together 1 star anise pod, broken into segments; 2 teaspoons Sichuan peppercorns; ¼ teaspoon fennel seeds; and ¼ teaspoon whole cloves. Mix in ¼ teaspoon ground cinnamon. Store in an airtight container in a dark place for up to 6 months.

CORNSTARCH Cornstarch, also known as cornflour, is used in many sauces for its thickening power. Just a few spoonfuls can change a thin liquid into a thick and shiny sauce. The starch is first blended with a small amount of liquid, allowing smooth blending into a larger amount of liquid. After adding the cornstarch mixture, let the sauce simmer for a few minutes, both to thicken it and to remove the chalky taste of the starch.

CORN SYRUP This commonly used sweetener is made from cornstarch. It comes in both dark and light versions, with the darker version being more flavorful. Corn syrup does not crystallize when heated.

GARLIC Garlic seems made for grilled food. If you like garlic, use it liberally in sauces and marinades for poultry, pork, and fish and seafood. A garlic press is a handy tool, especially when you are going to add garlic to a marinade. Choose firm, plump heads of garlic and store them in a cool, dry place. Reddish-skinned garlic from Mexico is one of the most flavorful varieties.

GARLIC POWDER Dried, powdered garlic is used in many spice rubs and is a good addition to the pantry. Buy it in small amounts and discard it after a few months, as garlic powder oxidizes easily and loses flavor. Dried, granulated garlic may be substituted.

GINGER Fresh ginger enlivens many Asian sauces, salads, and marinades. Peel ginger and chop it finely before using in a recipe.

GRILL BASKET Made in a variety of shapes and sizes, with a pair of hinged wire grids that can be latched shut, these baskets simplify grilling delicate foods like large fish fillets or whole fish, which can sometimes stick to the grill rack and fall apart when turned. Use them, too, for grilling small foods such as shrimp, cherry tomatoes, and asparagus that otherwise might fall through the rack into the fire. Choose grill baskets with long, heatproof handles to facilitate safe turning. To help prevent sticking, brush the inside surfaces of baskets with oil before adding the food.

GRILL BRUSH Designed for cleaning grills, this long-handled brush has rust-proof bristles and a stainless-steel scraper. Use it while the grill is still hot after cooking to scrape off any food particles stuck to the rack.

GRILLING PLATES Perforated metal plates with small holes are often used to grill small pieces of seafood, fish, or vegetables to prevent them from falling through the grill. These come in a variety of shapes and sizes. Oil before using.

HERBS Fresh or dried herbs provide flavor and interest to many grilled foods. Use fresh herbs to season pastes, sauces, and marinades. Dried herbs are best in spice rubs, especially if you intend to store them for any time. Use twice as much fresh herbs as dry.

OIL Many recipes in this book call for vegetable oil to prevent food from sticking to the grill. A blended oil or pure corn oil is a good choice. Olive oil has an excellent flavor; extra-virgin has the deepest color and flavor, pure olive oil the lightest. Use flavorful oils in salads and sauces, lighter oils for coating foods and cooking. Peanut oil has a light nutty flavor much prized by Asian cooks. Sesame oil has a distinct, toasty flavor and should be added with restraint to Asian style sauces and salads. Canned oil sprays are very handy for grilling. Use them to oil the grill before it is heated and to coat fish, seafood, vegetables, and less-fatty meats and poultry before grilling.

PANCETTA A flavorful, unsmoked Italian bacon, pancetta is made from the same cut, pork belly, as the more common bacon, but it is salt-cured instead of smoked and has a subtler taste. It is rubbed with a mix of spices that may include cinnamon, cloves, or juniper berries, then rolled into a tight cylinder and cured for at least 2 months. Look for good domestic brands of pancetta at delicatessens and Italian markets.

PAPRIKA Made from ground dried red peppers and ranging from orange-red to red, paprika is used both as a garnish and as a flavoring. Hungary makes the finest paprika. Three basic types are available: sweet, half-sweet, and hot. Sweet paprika is the most commonly used.

SOY SAUCE This pungent, salty sauce, made from fermented soy beans, comes in various types and textures. Soy sauce ranges from light to deep, dark, and intense. Use the style you prefer in sauces and marinades. Low-sodium soy sauce is widely available. Tamari is a delicious soy sauce with a deep, complex flavor.

SPARK LIGHTER Many gas grills come equipped with a spark igniter. If you don't have one, use a long match or gas wand. If the burners do not ignite immediately when using a spark lighter, turn off the burners, wait 5 or more minutes, then light with a long match.

THERMOMETERS An instant-read thermometer will let you measure the doneness of large cuts of meat or poultry quickly. Inserted near the end of cooking, instant-read thermometers are more accurate and make smaller holes in the meat, and thus release less juices, than other types of meat thermometers. When testing for doneness, be sure that the thermometer is not touching a bone, and do not leave the thermometer in the food while it is still on the grill. For long cooking with lower heat, if your covered grill doesn't come with a built-in thermometer, insert an instant-read thermometer in the vent opening to monitor the temperature inside without opening the lid. A grill thermometer attaches to a grill rack to measure surface temperature.

TONGS No grill cook should be without extra-long tongs for placing foods on the grill such as chicken, spareribs, and sausages; turning them; and removing them quickly when they are done without piercing them and losing juices. A second pair of tongs is especially useful for rearranging or moving hot coals.

WHITE PEPPER Hulled black pepper provides a light and delicate flavor and is especially nice with fish or seafood.

WORCESTERSHIRE SAUCE A traditional English seasoning or condiment, Worcestershire sauce is an intensely flavorful, savory, and aromatic blend of many ingredients, including molasses, soy sauce, garlic, onion, and anchovies. Popular in marinades for grilled foods, it can also be passed at the table.

SIMON & SCHUSTER SOURCE
A Division of Simon & Schuster Inc.
Rockefeller Center
1230 Avenue of the Americas
New York, NY 10020

WILLIAMS-SONOMA
Founder and Vice-Chairman: Chuck Williams
Book Buyer: Cecilia Michaelis

WELDON OWEN INC.
Chief Executive Officer: John Owen
President: Terry Newell
Chief Operating Officer: Larry Partington
Vice President, International Sales: Stuart Laurence
Creative Director: Gaye Allen
Series Editor: Sarah Putman Clegg
Associate Editor: Heather Belt
Production Manager: Chris Hemesath
Photograph Editor: Lisa Lee

Weldon Owen wishes to thank the following
people for their generous assistance and support in
producing this book: Copy Editor Carolyn Miller;
Consulting Editors Sharon Silva and Norman Kolpas;
Designer Douglas Chalk; Food Stylist Sandra Cook;
Photographer's Assistant Noriko Akiyama; Assistant
Food Stylists Jennifer McConnell, Elisabet der
Nederlanden, and Ann Tonai; Assistant Photograph
Editor Kris Ellis; Proofreaders Desne Ahlers and
Carrie Bradley; Indexer Ken DellaPenta; and
Production Designer Joan Olson.

Williams-Sonoma Collection *Grilling* was
conceived and produced by Weldon Owen Inc.,
814 Montgomery Street, San Francisco,
California 94133, in collaboration with
Williams-Sonoma, 3250 Van Ness Avenue,
San Francisco, California 94109.

A Weldon Owen Production
Copyright © 2002 by Weldon Owen Inc. and
Williams-Sonoma Inc.

Set in Trajan, Utopia, and Vectora.

Color separations by Bright Arts Graphics
Singapore (Pte.) Ltd.
Printed and bound in Singapore by Tien Wah
Press (Pte.) Ltd.

For information about special discounts for bulk
purchases, please contact Simon & Schuster
Special Sales: 1-800-456-6798 or
business@simonandschuster.com

First printed in 2002.

10 9 8 7 6 5 4 3 2

Library of Congress Cataloging-in-Publication Data
Kelly, Denis, 1939–
   Grilling / recipes and text, Denis Kelly ; general
editor, Chuck Williams ; photographs, Noel
Barnhurst.
       p. cm. — (Williams-Sonoma collection)
   Includes index.
   1. Barbecue cookery. I. Title: At head of title:
Williams-Sonoma. II. Title: Williams-Sonoma
Grilling. III. Williams, Chuck. IV. Title. V. Williams-
Sonoma collection (New York, N.Y.)
TX840 .B3 K435 2002
641.7'6—dc21
                                      2001042918
ISBN 0-7432-2642-9

A NOTE ON WEIGHTS AND MEASURES

All recipes include customary U.S. and metric measurements. Metric conversions are based on
a standard developed for these books and have been rounded off. Actual weights may vary.